Coaching Baseball Effectively

The American Coaching Effectiveness Program
Level 1 Baseball Book

Steven D. Houseworth, PhD
American Coaching Effectiveness Program

Human Kinetics Publishers, Inc.
Champaign, Illinois

Library of Congress Cataloging-in-Publication Data

Houseworth, Steven D., 1955-
  Coaching baseball effectively.

  1. Baseball—coaching.   2. Baseball for children—
Coaching.   I. Title.
GV875.5H68   1986   796.357'07'7   85-24836
ISBN 0-87322-037-4

Production director: Ernest Noa
Copy editor: Olga Murphy
Design: Julie Szamocki
Typesetter: Sandra Meier
Text layout: Denise Mueller
Illustrator: Dick Flood
Cover design: Jack W. Davis
Printed by: Phillips Brothers

ISBN 0-87322-037-4

Printed in the United States of America

10 9 8 7 6 5 4 3

Human Kinetics Publishers, Inc.
Box 5076, Champaign, IL 61825-5076
1-800-747-4457

Canada Office:
Human Kinetics Publishers, Inc.
P.O. Box 2503, Windsor, ON N8Y 4S2
1-800-465-7301 (in Canada only)

UK Office:
Human Kinetics Publishers (UK) Ltd.
P.O. Box 18
Rawdon, Leeds LS19 6TG
England
(0532) 504211

Series Preface

Coaching Baseball Effectively is part of the American Coaching Effectiveness Program (ACEP) Level 1 sport-specific series. The decision to produce this series evolved after the release of the ACEP Level 1 sport science course. In that course local youth sport administrators were encouraged to apply the information presented to the specific sports in their program. They were asked to identify the skills to be taught and the proper progression in teaching these skills. They were also asked to develop a seasonal plan and sample practice plans for their coaches.

The task seemed easy enough, but it was not. Considerable time is needed to carefully identify the skills to be taught and then to put them into a seasonal plan from which daily practice plans can be derived. As a result, the ACEP staff were encouraged to develop this information for various sports which we now have done.

The ACEP LEVEL 1 sport-specific series is unique in several ways.

1. The emphasis is on *teaching* skills to athletes, not on how to learn the skills yourself, as in most other books.
2. The emphasis also is on teaching basic skills to beginning athletes. Often, they will be very young children, but not always. Therefore, the books in this series are developed for coaches who teach the basics to children from 6 to 15 years of age.
3. Careful consideration is given to the proper *progression* for teaching these skills. Information from the field of motor development is combined with the practical experience of veteran coaches to ensure that the progressions maximize learning and minimize the risk of injury.
4. *Seasonal* plans for the teaching of basic skills are presented along with *daily practice plans* for three age groups. Coaches will find these plans very helpful.
5. Drills or exercises appropriate for beginning athletes are also included.

Three other helpful features appear in each book in this series: A short history of the sport to help you appreciate the evolution of the game, a glossary of terms, and the rules of the sport are provided.

Being *practical, basic*, and *accurate* were the guiding principles in preparing this series. The content had to be practical for beginning coaches and yet equally useful for more experienced coaches. Coaches did not need another treatise on the sport; many of those are already available.

Keeping this series basic was perhaps the most difficult task. Including more information about the skills to impress coaches with all the knowledge available was constantly tempting. However, we resisted because this is not what coaches of beginning athletes need.

Finally, accuracy was essential; thus, many expert coaches and sport scientists reviewed the content of the book to confirm its accuracy.

To achieve maximum benefit, the books in this series cannot be read in an evening and then be put aside. They must be used like a reference book, a dictionary, or a working manual. Read the book thoroughly; then refer to it often during the season.

C1

This book and ACEP are dedicated to the purpose of improving the quality of youth sports. We hope you will find the books in the series useful to you in achieving that goal. Enjoy your coaching, and thanks for helping young people learn to play sports better.

Rainer Martens, PhD
ACEP Founder

Contents

List of Drills

Preface

After presenting the ACEP Level 1 sport medicine and science program across the country over the past few years, one comment has been repeatedly expressed by youth sport coaches and administrators: "A sport specific book incorporating the ACEP philosophy and principles of teaching would really help our program."

Novice coaches wanted a guide to help them understand how to teach skills to players rather than a book that simply showed how to perform skills. Experienced coaches wanted a guide with practical drills and hints for improving their coaching skills. Administrators asked where to find a book that showed coaches who have full-time jobs and family responsibilities how to plan practices throughout a season and how to conduct daily practice sessions without spending hours in this process. In reply to these coaches and administrators, this sport specific book includes these features and more.

Coaches will benefit from the practical and easy-to-use style in which the book is written, explaining *how to teach* baseball skills to beginning players. Included in these explanations are (a) *coaching points*, indicating common errors and areas of emphasis specific to beginning players; (b) *teaching progressions*, specifying effective teaching strategies for proper skill development; and (c) *practice drills*, focusing on rehearsing skill basics and playing principles necessary for effective baseball play.

However, while writing the early drafts of *Coaching Baseball Effectively*, I quickly realized that this book needed one additional feature: It must be easy to use, or said in today's computer

jargon, it must be "user friendly." This ease of use is reflected in several ways. First, the book is divided into two main parts: *The Baseball Coaching Guide*, which presents how to teach baseball skills, and *The Baseball Planning Guide*, which presents instructional schedules, daily practice plans, and other materials essential to coaching a team.

Second, practice drills are referenced and explained chapter by chapter and are labeled according to the chapter and sequence in which they are presented. You will find *Drill (5.3)* by turning to the Drills section in chapter 5 and locating the third drill listed. Each drill is also referenced in the List of Drills at the front of this book. Use this list if you remember the name of a specific drill but cannot remember the number for that drill.

Third, several tools located in the appendices will help you implement the material presented in this book. These tools are (a) sample outlines for developing your own instructional guides and daily practice plans, (b) simplified baseball rules, (c) evaluation forms to help you chart the skill development of your players as well as your performance as a coach, and (d) a glossary of baseball terms.

No other youth sport in the United States is as popular as baseball. From 5-year-olds who can barely swing a bat to 18-year-olds executing hit and runs, baseball is the king of youth sports. I remember with mixed emotions my early years playing baseball. Some coaches were very good at teaching skills, and some were not. Some made practices fun while showing me how to work hard—those practices always ended too soon. Other coaches made practices sheer drudgery—worse than mowing the lawn. Consequently, I played ball as poorly as I mowed and never looked forward to the next game when I would sit on the bench. Reflecting back, the best coaches were not always highly skilled players. Instead, they were skilled communicators, impressing in my mind how to swing a bat level and how to move in line with a ball I would field. Not only did those coaches help me play better baseball then, but they have also helped me play better recreational softball now as an adult. It is true for all of us that our everyday experiences are constant reminders of the attitudes and skills developed through youth sports.

Thus, this book was written to help you be an effective communicator as well as to take the guesswork out of your coaching. Rather than your athletes *accidentally* learning baseball skills, this book will help you make *certain* they learn baseball skills. I hope you will study it carefully and apply the information you learn from it, helping your players to learn skills and to enjoy their time with you. As a result, you will enjoy coaching more, knowing you have done your best for each player now and in the future.

We at ACEP are pleased to follow Bragg Stockton's *Coaching Baseball: Skills and Drills* with this book written for baseball coaches of beginning players. Serving as our technical consultant, Bragg Stockton provided the insight and information that make this book thorough in baseball content, thus providing a base from which coaches may gain knowledge for teaching and demonstrating baseball skills. As you and your players become more experienced, this information will help you present the advanced baseball skills found in *Coaching Baseball: Skills and Drills*.

Steve Houseworth
Curriculum Development Director
Sport-Specific Program
American Coaching Effectiveness Program

Baseball
Coaching Guide

Welcome to Baseball! You have joined the estimated 3 million other coaches who make youth sports possible in the United States. Whether you are a volunteer or a paid coach, you have the opportunity to make a tremendous contribution to the development of your young athletes. Furthermore, almost 5 million young people participate annually in youth baseball, making it America's most popular youth sport.

People coach for many different reasons: Some coach because they love sports; some because they enjoy working with young people. Others coach because they have a son or daughter who will play on the team. These are all good reasons to coach youth baseball. In fact, no matter why you choose to coach, taking the time to help young athletes learn baseball is an important contribution to their development and, consequently, to your community.

So now you are facing the upcoming baseball season. Have you coached baseball before? Have you thought about what you plan to do? Have you ever worked with beginning players? Do you know how to teach specific baseball skills? If the answer to any of these questions is no, then you will want to read this book carefully. If you are determined to help the beginning players on your team have a positive and successful baseball experience, and if you take the time to study *Coaching Baseball Effectively*, then you will be on your way to a successful season.

It is important for every coach to establish a coaching philosophy, for this philosophy will help you determine (a) your goals, or what you want to accomplish, and (b) how you will accomplish these goals. You may want to consider one of two major coaching philosophies: You might choose to emphasize winning as the most important objective, or you might stress participation, fun, and skill development as the most important objective.

The philosophy we advocate through the American Coaching Effectiveness Program is *Athletes First—Winning Second*. By this statement we mean that every decision you make as a coach should first be in the best interest of your athletes, and second in the desire to win. We hope that helping young people to develop physically, psychologically, and socially will always be more important to you as you coach than beating the other team.

Athletes First—Winning Second does not mean winning is unimportant, or said more accurately, that striving to win is unimportant. You should instill in your players a desire to win, to do their best, to pursue excellence. However, the outcome of the game—the winning or losing—is not the most important objective. The most important objective is that your players try to win, that they try their best. If they do their best, they will have been successful—regardless of the outcome of the contest.

This philosophy also will be reflected in how you present yourself to the players on your team. As a coach, you are in an influential position. Thus, *how* you teach will be as important as *what* you teach. To implement the ACEP philosophy, consider the following points:

Be a good role model. Present a model for behavior you want your athletes to emulate. Set positive examples at practices and games.

Everyone is important. Treat each player as an important human being. Each player will have a different personality and different needs. Be sensitive to these differences and show interest and concern for each team member.

Consider the age and skill levels of your players. Your athletes will be full of energy and eager to try many skills. However, they are also young and not yet capable of performing as adults. This means you must approach your athletes at *their* level. Do not expect them to come up to your level.

Consider individual differences. Teach beginning baseball skills according to the ability of each player. Some players will be fast learners with whom you can progress rapidly. Other players will not learn as quickly, so you will need to proceed more slowly with them.

Keep everyone active. Organize your practices and games so that each player is able to participate as much as possible. Young players want to play baseball for many reasons; one of the most important reasons is to have fun participating. If they are not kept active in practices or allowed to play in games, they will quickly lose interest.

Include athletes in the decision-making process. Young athletes should have input as to what skills they practice and as to how they practice them. Ask your players what they need to work on, how they want to be grouped for practice, and what positions they would like to play. Naturally, young athletes should not control the entire practice, but do consider their interests and ideas when designing practices and playing games.

4

Be patient. You will need to have patience with beginning players who are learning baseball. Baseball skills require timing, coordination, and glove control that can only be developed through repeated practice. Encourage your players to develop their skills, and positively reinforce players for their effort and skill development. When young players learn new skills, both you and your players should be proud.

Part I:
Offensive Play

Your players will enjoy hitting balls, running the bases, and scoring runs. It is a deeply satisfying feeling to hit a solid line drive to center field and reach base safely. But your players must also be prepared to experience striking out, hitting into a double play, and being thrown out while attempting to stretch a single into a double. Being put out will not be much fun, but it is part of the game, and your players must understand that reaching a base safely does not happen each time at bat. Helping your players develop realistic goals about their offensive achievements is as important as teaching them basic offensive skills.

This section presents the offensive skills of hitting and baserunning, and explains how to teach these skills to your baseball players more effectively. By following the techniques, teaching strategies, and drills listed in this section, you can increase the fun of hitting, running, and scoring; you will also help your players from becoming too discouraged when they are put out.

Chapter 1: Batting

Introduction: Hitting the Ball

Hitting a small round ball flying through the air with a slender, rounded stick is one of the most difficult skills in sport. It is a skill that requires good hand-eye coordination and visual judgment. Hitting can be highly enjoyable when these components are well developed but can be frustrating when they are not. To help you teach hitting skills properly, the following topics are explained in this chapter:

- The bat
- The grip
- The stance
- The swing
- Conditioning exercises for batting
- Bunting
- Batting drills

Several drills which will help your players practice effective batting mechanics are the Swinging in Front of a Mirror Drill (1.1), the Wiffle or Sock Ball on a String Drill (1.2), the Hitting off a Tee Drill (1.3), the Swinging a Bat Drill (1.4), and the Hitting Easy Pitches Drill (1.5).

The Bat

Present the bat to your players and explain that it is divided into three parts: the *knob*, the *handle*, and the *barrel* as illustrated in Figure 1-1.

Tell your athletes that bats usually have a number that indicates the length (in inches) of

Fig. 1-1

KNOB   HANDLE   BARREL

the bat printed on the end of the knob. For wooden bats, this number is also a good indication of the bat's weight. For example, if a wooden bat has the number 28 stamped on the end of the knob, this means the bat is 28 in. long and will probably be close to 28 oz in weight. Metal bats will have the length stamped on the end of the knob or on the barrel of the bat. However, the length of a metal bat does not always indicate its weight. Be sure you instruct your players to look for the printed weight and length if they select metal bats.

Bat Safety

Bats, of course, must be safe. Baseball rules state the bat should be all-wood or all-metal. Wooden bats should be hardened and finished, not rough. Metal bats must be one piece or have a plug in the barrel end. If a bat does not have a plug in the end, it is dangerous and should not be used, not even in practices. The knob on a metal bat should be a continuation of the handle. Some older metal bats have a rubber knob plugged into the handle; this type of bat is illegal, unsafe, and should *never* be used. The distinctions between legal and illegal metal bats are shown in Figure 1-2.

Fig. 1-2

LEGAL BAT

ONE-PIECE CONSTRUCTION   END PLUG

ILLEGAL BAT

PLUG HANDLE   NO END PLUG

Selecting The Proper Bat

Help your players select bats that are the proper length and weight for their body size and strength (see Figure 1-3). The most important selection criterion is that the bat feels comfortable and is easy to swing. Tell your players that the length and weight of a bat will affect their swing: A heavy bat may cause a slow, jerky swing; a bat that is too light may cause an early swing. The bat should be long enough to touch the outside corner of the plate when the player stands in the batter's box.

Fig. 1-3

The Grip

After helping your players select the bat, demonstrate how to use it properly. First, tell your players to grip the bat as though they were shaking hands with it; right-handed hitters place the left hand against the knob, with the right

hand on top of the left hand; left-handed hitters place the right hand against the knob, with the left hand on top of the right hand. The bat should fit in the hands comfortably but firmly, with the fingers spread slightly apart and the thumbs at the top of each hand as shown in Figure 1-4.

Fig. 1-4

RIGHT-HANDED BATTER

LEFT-HANDED BATTER

Choking up on the Bat

It is doubtful that the bats provided to you will be the ideal size and weight for all of your players. Batters may gain more control by *choking up* on the bat as shown in Figure 1-5, which means moving the batter's grip up on the handle, or toward the barrel. Choking up will

Fig. 1-5

help those players who lack sufficient strength to swing the bat quickly and accurately. Players can choke up slightly or quite a bit. Teach each player how to choke up and let each one find the grip that works best.

Coaching Points for the Grip

1. Shake hands with the bat.
2. Grip the bat with both hands close together.
3. Grip the bat firmly, yet keep it flexible.
4. Adjust the grip by choking up on the bat handle.

The Stance

The *stance*, or the position the batter takes in the batter's box, is the next step in teaching good hitting skills. This is the foundation of hitting and must be mastered in order to hit well. The stance has many components and should be taught simply, especially to beginning players who are just learning the game. The simpler and clearer the explanation, the easier it will be to master the stance.

Selecting a Batting Stance

The *open, closed,* and *square* stances are the three general batting stances used in baseball (see Figure 1-6). In an *open* stance, the batter stands with the front foot toward the outside of the batter's box. This stance can help batters in three ways. First, because the front foot is positioned toward the outside of the batter's box, the open stance helps batters who tend to step toward the inside of the batter's box by forcing

Fig. 1-6

CLOSED STANCE

SQUARE STANCE   OPEN STANCE

the front foot to step more toward the pitcher than toward home plate. Second, the open stance helps batters contact the ball earlier, or sooner, than other stances. This means the open stance is useful when the batter is up against fast pitchers or has a relatively late (slow) swing. Third, this stance helps batters hit the ball along the baseline from their batting side (e.g., right-handed batters hit along the third baseline; left-handed batters hit along the first baseline).

The *closed* stance positions the front foot toward the inside of the batter's box and is used for the opposite reasons of the open stance. First, the closed stance will help correct batters who tend to step toward the outside of the batter's box. Second, this stance helps batters who swing too early (fast) or who face a relatively slow pitcher. Third, the closed stance will help batters "pull" the ball or hit toward the opposite field from which they bat (e.g., a right-handed batter pulls toward left field; a left-handed batter pulls toward right field).

The most desirable batting stance is the *square* stance. In this stance the feet are aligned, the toes point squarely toward home plate, and the batter steps directly toward the pitcher rather than toward the outside or inside of the batter's box. This stance is useful for players who have a well-timed batting swing and who want to hit the ball toward the middle part of the field (between the shortstop's and the second baseman's positions).

Most beginning players will not use the same stance each time, so you will need to watch your players closely and alter ineffective stances. Also, some players may naturally use an open or closed stance, so let your players try batting in the stance that is most natural to them. If they have difficulty hitting from the natural stance, you can then adjust the stance until they are able to hit well. When you alter a player's stance, do not use an exaggerated open or closed position. This would be uncomfortable and probably cause more problems than it solves. Instead, alter the batting position bit by bit until your player can bat effectively.

The Shoulders and Arms

The position of the shoulders and arms will naturally follow the position of the feet. For example, an open stance will cause the shoulders to be open, and a closed stance will cause the shoulders to be closed, as illustrated in Figure 1-7.

Fig. 1-7

Regardless of the stance used, the arms need to be held comfortably back, about shoulder height, and slightly away from the shoulders. From this position it is difficult to rest the bat on the back shoulder. (This is a bad habit and should be discouraged.)

The Head and Eyes

Unless your players are lucky, they will not hit what they cannot see. Therefore, demonstrate how to watch the ball throughout the swing (see Figure 1-8). Jerking the head as the batter starts the swing is a frequent cause of batters not following the ball as it approaches the plate.

Fig. 1-8

Position in the Batter's Box

Whatever stance your batters choose, have them stand back in the box so the front foot is even with the back corner of home plate and they can touch the far front corner with the bat (see Figure 1-9). Standing back in the box increases the chance of hitting the ball because the batter has a little more time to react to the pitch. As your players acquire a "feel" for batting, this position should be adjusted according to the speed of each pitcher and to where the batter wants to hit the ball.

Fig. 1-9

Coaching Points for the Stance

1. Position the feet about hip-width apart and square to the plate.
2. Stand away from the plate so that the bat touches the far corner.
3. Stand back in the batter's box; keep the front foot even with the back corner of home plate.
4. Hold the shoulders square and the arms comfortably back.
5. Watch the ball.

The Swing

Now you are ready to explain the three phases of the batting swing: the *stride*, the *arm motion*, and the *follow-through*. To hit a ball with a slender bat, these movements must be precisely timed and coordinated. Also, because the swing is a difficult skill to teach, be patient with your players and practice the drills suggested in this chapter, including the Batting/Fielding Drill (1.6), which is helpful for practicing the batting swing in game situations.

Stride

Beginning baseball players often think the most important part of batting is swinging the bat with the arms. However, because the stride moves the body into a swinging position, it is equally as important as the swing.

During the stride, the front foot steps toward the pitcher and the body weight shifts forward, providing the batter power. This stride does not need to be long; about 6 to 12 in. will give the batter plenty of power without losing control of the bat (see Figure 1-10). Be sure to emphasize that the stride is a smooth and deliberate step, not a fast or jerky step.

Fig. 1-10

STRIDE 6 TO 12 INCHES

The Arm Motion

When the front foot is planted, the stride ends and the forward arm swing begins: The arms should swing the bat smooth and level as the hips and chest turn toward the pitcher (see Figure 1-11).

Fig. 1-11

When demonstrating the arm swing, show how to extend the arms (straighten the elbows) because some players may tend to keep their elbows bent. If the elbows are bent, the bat will probably not reach across the plate to hit the ball, and it will be difficult to swing the bat level or with power.

The Wrist Action
Wrist action is an important part of the batting swing. Because it is a natural part of the swing, it should be presented and practiced slowly. For proper wrist action, the wrists should rotate or "break" in the middle of the swing, as shown in Figure 1-12. Demonstrate how this breaking of

Fig. 1-12

the wrists occurs as the bat contacts the ball. Practicing the Wrist Roller Drill (1.7), located at

the end of this chapter, will help batters learn to rotate the wrists and to develop a good arm swing.

Contacting the Ball
The arm motion does not end with the bat hitting the ball; your players should try to hit *through* the ball. Tell your players hitting through the ball means trying to slice the ball in half so that the bat will be on the other side of the ball.

The Follow-Through

The follow-through is the final part of the swing and is the result of a good stride and proper arm action. During this phase the wrists continue to rotate, the arms swing across the body, and the hips twist fully around (see Figure 1-13). Sometimes players are afraid to swing hard, or hit through the ball, because they do not know how to follow through properly and because the bat hurts the arm or shoulder when it comes around. By developing a proper follow-through, batters can hit through the ball powerfully without hurting the arms.

Fig. 1-13

Coaching Points for the Swing

1. Stride with the front foot 6 to 12 in. toward the pitcher.
2. Focus the eyes on the ball.
3. Swing the arms level.
4. Swing through the ball.
5. Follow through.

Teaching Progression for the Swing

1. Teach the stride.
2. Combine the stride with the arm swing.
3. Combine the stride, arm swing, and follow-through.

Conditioning Exercises for Batting

Having the strength to swing bats and hit baseballs effectively is important for several reasons: Insufficient strength to grip the bat firmly and to swing the bat correctly will impair a player's ability to learn batting skills effectively and thus increase the chance for injury. To bat effectively, batters need a combination of leg, trunk, and arm strength that can be developed by performing the following conditioning exercises:

Bat Lifts

Have your players grip a bat with the hand just above the knob and hold it out in front of the body. Then move the bat up and down with the wrists only, as shown in Figure 1-14. This is also a good choking-up exercise to demonstrate because if a bat is too heavy, the player can choke up, making the bat easier to lift.

Fig. 1-14

Squeezing Tennis Balls

Grip strength can be developed by squeezing tennis balls, racquet balls, or any other soft, rubber balls. Be sure to exercise both hands because both hands are used in batting.

Resistance Arm Swings

Have players work in pairs, as shown in Figure 1-15. One player swings a bat against the resistance of a partner holding the bat (see Figure 1-15). The player swinging the bat should start in the ready position and swing the bat while the other player applies resistance. The amount of resistance depends upon the strength of the batter; it should be enough to make the batter work, but should not prevent the batter from swinging smoothly.

Fig. 1-15

Bat Weights

Another method of improving batting strength is to use a bat weight. Bat weights can be slipped over a bat to increase resistance during the swing and to develop strength. Because a weighted bat may alter a batter's swing, emphasize using proper swinging technique. Also, make sure the bat weights will not fly off.

Hip Twists

This exercise will be fun as well as beneficial. Have players stand with their legs about hip-width apart, arms held to the side, and twist the body from side to side as shown in Figure 1-16.

Fig. 1-16

General Exercises

In addition to the exercises listed above, general conditioning exercises such as push-ups and sit-ups will help your players develop strength in the shoulders and stomach. These general conditioning exercises are useful because the muscles of the shoulders and stomach are used to support and stabilize the arms and body when batting.

Bunting

Explain to your players that bunting is a way to hit the ball very softly. Bunting is not an easy skill for beginning players, but it is effective because the ball is hit slowly, causing fielders to run in to field the ball rather than waiting for the ball to come to them. To help your players learn this difficult but effective skill, follow the coaching points and teaching progressions presented below and practice by using the Bunt Drill (1.8).

You can demonstrate and teach the bunt, as shown in Figures 1-17 to 1-20, by (a) turning from the batting stance to face the pitcher squarely (be sure both feet remain inside the

Fig. 1-17   **Fig. 1-18**   **Fig. 1-19**

Fig. 1-20

batter's box), (b) sliding the top hand up to the barrel of the bat, (c) holding the bat with the top hand between the thumb and the index finger (with all other fingers bent behind the bat), and (d) placing the bat in a level position in front of the pitch. Tell your players to bunt softly as if trying to catch the ball with the bat.

Placing the Bunt

As your players become more proficient at bunting, encourage them to "place" bunts by learning to direct the ball to a specific area. For example, to bunt toward third base, the bat should be turned toward third base; to bunt toward first base, the bat should be turned toward first base (see Figure 1-21).

Fig. 1-21

Coaching Points for the Bunt

1. Be sure the batter is in a square stance facing the pitcher.
2. Check the grip. The lower hand should grip the handle; the upper hand should grip the barrel of the bat between the thumb and the forefinger.
3. Be sure the bunter holds the bat level with the ground.
4. Raise and lower the bat by moving up and down with the legs.
5. Emphasize trying to catch the ball with the bat.

Teaching Progression for the Bunt

1. Demonstrate and practice how to hold the bat in a bunt position.
2. Teach your players how to square up to the pitcher and assume the bunt position.
3. Practice bunting easy pitches from a moderate distance.
4. Gradually progress to bunting balls thrown at regular pitching speed from the regulation pitching distance.
5. Practice placing bunts.
6. Practice bunting under game conditions.

Batting Drills

(1.1) Swinging in Front of a Mirror Drill

Age: 9 years and up

Purpose: To allow players to observe their batting mechanics

Equipment: Mirror, bats (optional—can be performed at home without bats)

Procedure: Players stand in front of a mirror and swing as if hitting a ball. Instruct them to concentrate on the position of their arms, legs, head, and shoulders.

(1.2) Whiffle or Sock Ball on a String Drill

Age: 9 years and up

Purpose: To help your players learn to keep their heads still and their eyes on the ball when swinging

Equipment: Bat, whiffle ball, or sock ball (old socks tied into knots the size of a ball), a baseball tied to a rope

Procedure: Suspend the sock ball or ball on a rope from a garage ceiling, backstop overhang, or any other apparatus that will allow your players to swing at the ball without interference. Players get into the ready position and practice hitting the ball correctly.

(1.3) Hitting Off a Tee Drill

Age: All

Purpose: To develop the mechanics of players' swings using a stationary ball

Equipment: Batting tee, bats, baseballs, home plates

Procedure: Your players can construct a "hitting laboratory" in a garage or on the field. Balls can be hit into a net, tarp, sheet, backstop, or blanket draped from the ceiling. Place the balls on the hitting tee and practice the batting swing.

(1.4) Swinging a Bat Drill

Age: All

Purpose: To develop and to refine a player's batting swing

Equipment: A bat (optional)

Procedure: Demonstrate how to (a) stride, (b) swing, and (c) follow through without the bat. Have your players practice these three phases and give them appropriate feedback to correct errors.

(1.5) Hitting Easy Pitches Drill

Age: All

Purpose: To practice hitting a pitched ball

Equipment: 3 balls, a bat, and a fence, backstop, or netting

Procedure: This drill is designed for paired players. One player tosses pitches while the other player bats. Position the batter so the ball is hit into a fence, net, or backstop. Position the pitcher about 10 ft away and at a 45° angle to the batter. This position will allow the pitcher to toss easy underhand pitches to the batter, who can hit the ball into the fence or net.

(1.6) Batting/Fielding Drill

Age: 9 years and up

Purpose: To develop batting skills and to help fielders react to hit balls

Equipment: Enough balls and bats to have batting practice; one complete set of bases

Procedure: Divide the team into batters and fielders. Have one batter and one "on-deck" batter. All other players are fielders. The coach or actual pitcher pitches 15 balls to each batter. The fielders should field the ball, throw to second base, to first base, and back to the pitcher. When a batter's turn is over, have him or her take a defensive position. The on-deck batter moves up to bat, and another fielder moves to the on-deck spot.

(1.7) Wrist Roller Drill

Age: 9 years and up

Purpose: To enhance bat control by strengthening the wrists

Equipment: Bats

Procedure: Have players get into a contact position and roll the bat forward and backward so that the bat touches each shoulder. Your players should use only their wrists and forearms to rotate the bat.

(1.8) Bunt Drill

Age: 9 years and up

Purpose: To develop the fundamentals of bunting

Equipment: A bat and ball for every two players

Procedure: Your players can work on bunting alone or with a partner. When alone, have them move from the batting stance to a square position with an imaginary pitcher; then hold the bat in the proper bunting position and punch at an imaginary pitched ball.

With a partner, the players alternate tossing pitches and bunting. One player stands about 15 to 20 ft from the other player and tosses easy pitches. The bunter should (a) assume the proper batting stance, (b) turn and squarely face the partner, (c) hold the bat in the proper bunt position, and (d) bunt the ball on the ground. After 10 to 12 bunts, players switch positions.

Chapter 2: Baserunning

Introduction: Speed and Control

The success of your players' baserunning will depend upon both their physical abilities and mental awareness. They must run as quickly as possible under control, know how to slide, avoid other players, and respond to instructions from the base coaches. Such a combination of all-out effort, field awareness, and body control makes baserunning a particularly difficult skill for beginning players. In this chapter the particular needs of young athletes for learning and for performing baserunning skills will be explained along with the following areas:

• Leaving the batter's box
• Running past first base
• Rounding the bases
• Coaching the bases
• Stealing bases
• Sliding
• Baserunning Drills

Leaving the Batter's Box

When a batter hits a pitched ball, he or she becomes a base runner and must run to first base. Teach your players to run out of the box as soon as they hit the ball. Young players tend to watch the ball after hitting it rather than immediately running for first base. The moments players spend watching a ball could be the difference between being safe or out. A good way to develop this skill is to practice the Leaving the Batter's Box Drill (2.1).

Even though your players may think they will be out on easy fly balls or other apparent easy outs, remind them that they are safe until the umpire calls them out, and that they should run through first base each time they hit a ball. If they develop the habit of running hard after each hit, they will have a better chance to beat any close plays.

How to Leave the Batter's Box

To leave the batter's box and run to first base, instruct your players to turn from the follow-through batting position and step toward first base, as shown in Figure 2-1. Some players may run the first few steps sideways, or they may criss-cross their legs. If this occurs, demonstrate how to look, turn, and step toward first base, as illustrated in Figure 2-2.

Fig. 2-1

Fig. 2-2

Fig. 2-3

Coaching Points for Leaving the Batter's Box

1. Run! Do not watch the ball.
2. Turn the head and step toward first base.

Running Past First Base

Explain that running to first base is an all-out sprint and that base runners can run past first base without being tagged out (see Figure 2-3). Therefore, teach your base runners to run as fast as possible until they are beyond first base. A useful strategy is to tell them not to start slowing down until they have taken at least one step beyond the base.

Even though they can run past first base, your players can be called out if they interfere with balls thrown to first base or with players fielding the ball. A good way to prevent interference calls and still reach first base quickly is to run along the baseline in foul territory rather than in fair territory (see Figure 2-3).

Also, as shown in Figure 2-4, young players tend to leap onto first base, which is not as fast as a running step. To reinforce these points, have your players practice the Running Past First

Fig. 2-4

Base Drill (2.2) described at the end of the chapter.

Coaching Points for Running Past First Base

1. Run as fast as possible.
2. Run past first base.
3. Step on the front side of first base.
4. Do not jump onto first base.

Rounding the Bases

Rounding First Base

When a ball has been hit to the outfield, runners may be able to run around first base and go to second base. Show your players how to run wide just before reaching first base; then show them how to angle toward the base, touching the inside corner of the bag, as shown in Figure 2-5, and how to run another two steps while listening (not looking) for instructions from the base coach. If the base coach calls out, "Go to second," the runner can proceed to second base; but if the base coach calls out, "Stop at first," the runner should return to first base. Use the Rounding First Base Drill (2.3) and the Running From Home Plate to First Base Drill (2.4) to practice running to and around first base.

Fig. 2-5

Rounding Second and Third Base

Rounding second base and third base is similar to rounding first base (see Figure 2-6). The player swings wide as he or she approaches the base, then angles in and touches the inside corner. To reinforce these points and to practice running around second and third base, use the Running the Bases Drill (2.5).

Remind your players that unlike running to first base, they can be tagged out if they run

Fig. 2-6

beyond second or third base. Base runners can keep from overrunning a base by sliding or by coming to a standing stop. Sliding, explained later in this chapter, is a good way to stop and avoid being tagged out.

Coaching Points for Rounding Bases

1. Look for and listen to the base coaches.
2. Swing outside of the base, angle toward the base, and touch the inside corner of the base.

Coaching the Bases

The importance of base coaches for an effective offense should not be overlooked. Coaching the bases is vital to a team's overall play and should be practiced just as your players practice baserunning. Both the first and third base coaches have two major responsibilities: (a) instructing the runner to remain at a base or advance to another, and (b) helping the runner leave the base. Many unnecessary errors are committed because runners are not told what to do, are told to do something they should not, or do not hear the base coach. Overcoming these problems is not easy. The job of basecoaching needs to be practiced as often as your players practice their skills.

When coaching the bases, keep these following points in mind:

• Get the runner's attention by calling out loud and clear.
• Know what you want the runner to do and do not hesitate to call out instructions.
• Use short, easy-to-understand phrases rather than long sentences.
• Play it safe and avoid unnecessary risks.

Coaching First Base

The decision to stay at first base or run to second depends on where the ball is hit and on the ability of the runner; the result will either be an extra base or an out. Consequently, we suggest you play it safe and hold the runner to the base if there is any doubt about reaching the next base.

You can use any system for telling players to stay at first base or to run to second. Some suggested phrases for the first base coach that are short and easy for beginners to understand are "Run through," "Round first," and "Take second" (see Figure 2-7). Verbal communication at first base is essential, because once the runner approaches first base, he or she should follow the instructions but not look for the base coach.

Fig. 2-7

"RUN THROUGH"

Coaching Second and Third Base

When runners are on second base or are running past second to third, teach them to *look* and *listen* to the third base coach for instructions. Wave your arms and call out whether they should (a) stop at second or third base, or (b) run to home plate (refer to Figure 2-8).

Fig. 2-8

"Hold at second"

Coaching Points for Base Coaching

1. Practice base coaching as your players practice baserunning.
2. Get the runner's attention and use short, clear statements.
3. Be cautious: Do not take unnecessary risks.

Running From a Base

In addition to teaching your players to run around the bases, you should teach them to (a) *lead off* a base, (b) return to a base, (c) *steal* a base, and (d) determine when to run or remain at a base following a hit. Remind your players that when they move off a base they can be put out, but when they are on a base, they are safe; therefore, they must always follow the directions of the base coaches. For the same reason your base coaches will need to communicate with the base runners at all times, telling them when and how far to lead off, when to run or steal, and when to remain on a base. Use the Base Start Drill (2.6) and the Leaving Bases Drill (2.7) to practice running from a base.

Leading Off

Explain to your players that base runners lead off by moving away from one base to get a good start toward the next base. Leading off (a) reduces the distance players actually run, (b) helps them reach the next base faster than standing on a base, (c) reduces the possibility of a double play, and (d) helps them distract the pitcher.

The best method for leading off a base is to use the side-step motion; this motion allows runners to remain balanced, mobile, and ready to run in either direction. Figure 2-9 shows how to use the side-step motion when leading off a base.

Fig. 2-9

After leading off the base, the runner gets set to run to the next base or return to the same base. Demonstrate this set position: Bend your legs slightly; position your feet about hip-width apart; bend the elbows; and hold your hands comfortably in front of your body, as illustrated in Figure 2-10.

Fig. 2-10

The actual distance players lead off will depend upon several factors, the most important being their speed and quickness. Runners who are fast and quick will be able to lead off farther than runners who are slower and not as quick. However, do not let any runner lead off too far. Be sure each player can return safely if a throw is made to the base he or she occupies.

The actual distance any runner can lead off will be learned through trial and error. It is a good idea to determine each player's lead-off during practices rather than during games. This will reduce the risk of mistakes during games and add confidence to a player's ability. To determine a lead-off distance, have each player take two side steps from first base, and return when the pitcher throws to first base. Next, have each player increase the lead by one-half step each time he or she returns to first base safely.

Coaching Points for Lead-Offs

1. Use the side-step motion to lead off.
2. Watch the pitcher.
3. Keep the legs bent and weight on the balls of the feet.
4. Hold the arms bent and relaxed.
5. Take a short lead-off initially and gradually increase the lead-off.

Returning to a Base

If the pitcher throws over to that base or if the pitch is not hit, the runner will need to return to the base. The two methods for returning to a base are (a) standing up and (b) diving. Demonstrate how to return standing up by using a crossover step and by touching the back side of the base with the foot, as illustrated in Figure 2-11. Explain that reaching for the back side of

Fig. 2-11

the base will make the defensive fielder reach farther and thus take longer to tag the runner.

Dive returns are used when the base runner is so far away that he or she cannot reach the base safely by standing up. However, a dive return can be dangerous, so warn your players about using it. If you do teach a dive return, wait until your players are about 12-years-old and are skilled enough to perform a dive correctly. By taking the time to determine each player's lead-off distance during practice, you will reduce the possibility of your players leading off too far, then needing to use the dive return.

The dive return is relatively simple to demonstrate. First, show your players how to use a crossover step and turn back toward the base, as shown in Figure 2-12. Second, show your players how to dive low and toward the back side of the base. The dive should be in a straight line rather than in a high arch (see Figure 2-13). A high dive increases the chance of injury and takes longer to reach the base. Be sure you demonstrate how to hold the arms a little wider than shoulder-width apart and how to use the hands to break the dive. Emphasize turning the head away from the tag to avoid being hit in the face.

Fig. 2-12

Fig. 2-13

Coaching Points for Returning to the Base

1. Teach players to return standing up.
2. Watch the pitcher.
3. Return to the base when the pitcher steps toward the base or steps off the pitching rubber.
4. Use a crossover step to turn toward the base.
5. Touch the back side of the base.

Teaching Progression for Leading Off and Returning to a Base

1. Teach the lead-off ready position.
2. Watch the pitcher.
3. Teach the side-step motion to lead off.
4. Teach the crossover step for returning to the base.
5. Teach the dive return when players are mature and skilled enough to properly execute a dive.

Running to the Next Base

If base runners do not return to the base they occupy, the only other option is to run to the next base. The method for running to the next base is similar to returning to a base standing up. Use a crossover step to turn toward the next base, then run straight ahead.

Coaching Points for Running to the Next Base

1. Watch the pitcher.
2. Use the side step to increase the lead-off.
3. Use the crossover step to turn and run.

Stealing Bases

Explain that stealing is running from one base to another without being tagged out. For example, Jason has taken a good lead off first base. When he sees the ball pitched to home plate, he turns and runs toward second base. If Jason reaches the base without being tagged with the ball, he is credited with a "steal." Remind your players that steals are very risky and should be attempted only when there is little possibility of being put out. Stealing is just like running from one base to another. From the lead-off position runners should use the crossover step and run toward the next base.

The most important aspect of stealing is knowing when to steal. Explain that if the runner tries to steal too soon, the pitcher can step back off the rubber and throw the runner out. If the runner tries to steal too late, the catcher will be able to throw the runner out. The right time to steal is when the pitcher begins to step toward home plate, as illustrated in Figure 2-14. Once the pitcher steps toward home plate, the pitch must be made, and the runner has a good chance of reaching the next base safely.

Fig. 2-14

Because young players may lack the speed and skills needed to steal bases, do not teach steals until your players are mature and skilled enough to execute them. Your judgment as a base coach is also important in steal situations. Be sure you and your base coaches tell each base runner when to run and when to remain at a base. Practicing the Lead-off, Running, and Steal Drill (2.8) will help you and your players develop these skills.

Coaching Points for Steals

1. Watch the pitcher.
2. Steal as soon as the pitcher strides toward home plate.
3. Use the crossover step to turn and run.

Baserunning Strategy

Simply teaching your players how to lead off, turn and run, and steal will not ensure they will be effective base runners. Your players must also be taught how, when, and why to remain at a base or when to run to the next base. This involves learning a few simple rules of baserunning strategy.

Rule 1: Watch the pitcher
Tell your players to watch the pitcher prepare to pitch the ball. If the pitcher strides toward home plate the ball cannot be thrown to the base, and the runner can increase the lead-off or try to steal. However, if the pitcher steps toward first base or the back foot steps off the rubber, your runner must return to the base.

Rule 2: Listen and watch the base coach
Tell your players that the base coach is on the field to watch all plays and to help them run safely. Therefore, runners on first base should listen to instructions from the first base coach; runners on second base should look for and listen to directions from the third base coach; and runners on third base should listen to instructions from the third base coach.

Rule 3: Do not run unless you are forced to run
Players are not always forced to run, and the base coach should tell the runner when a force is or is not in effect. For example, if a runner is on first base and a fly ball is caught, the runner is no longer forced to run to second base and can remain at first base.

Rule 4: Stay close to the base and tag up on fly balls
Remind your players that a caught fly ball is an automatic out. When a fly ball is caught, runners who have left a base must tag up and then run.

Coaching Points for Baserunning Strategy

1. Watch the pitcher.
2. Return to first base if the ball is not pitched.
3. Listen to the base coach.
4. Never run unless forced or can run to the next base safely.

Teaching Progression for Stealing and Baserunning Strategy

1. Teach players to use the crossover step.
2. Teach players to time the steal with the pitcher's stride toward home plate.
3. Teach the rules of baserunning strategy in order. Be sure each rule is understood and practiced before teaching the next rule.

Sliding

Sliding is an effective way for base runners to reach a base and avoid a tag, or to keep from running past the base. Actually, sliding is a controlled fall because the body glides over the top of the ground. It is a good idea not to teach sliding until players are about 10 years old, or until they are skilled enough to slide without being hurt. Sliding is difficult to learn and can be dangerous for unskilled or very young players. Because sliding is a controlled fall, it is a difficult skill to teach in stages. However, sliding can be taught while running slowly and progress to running faster.

The five basic slides are the *bent-leg* slide, the *stand-up* slide, the *decoy* slide, the *hook* slide, and the *head-first* slide. Do not teach all of these slides. Young players can easily injure themselves executing the head-first slide, stand-up slide, decoy slide, and hook slide. Teach only the bent-leg slide to your players and warn against the other slides. When the players are older, stronger, and more experienced, they will be able to learn and execute the other slides safely.

The Bent-Leg Slide

The bent-leg slide should start about 10 ft away from the base. To perform the bent-leg slide, show your base runners how to tuck one leg under the other leg, gently fall onto the bent leg, lean back, and sit down, as shown in Figure 2-15.

Then to maintain balance, show your players how to hold the arms comfortably up and to the side. Players should not place their hands on the

Fig. 2-15

ground, unless they lose control and begin to fall, because the hands and arms could become injured if slid across the ground.

Coaching Points for Sliding

1. Begin to slide about 10 ft from the base.
2. Tuck one leg under the other.
3. Lean back and sit down.
4. Keep arms held comfortably up off the ground.

Teaching Surfaces

Learning how to slide can be a great deal of fun for players if done in a safe environment. Water is a good teaching aid for presenting this skill. (Youngsters especially enjoying getting wet.) Players should be barefoot and wear either bathing suits or shorts and T-shirts.

Obtain long sheets of strong plastic (easily available as weatherproofing for windows); lay out these plastic sheets on grass fields that are free of ruts, rocks, or any other hazards, and then hose down the plastic. (This surface really encourages sliding.) Have your players run on grass up to the plastic sheet and slide; but do not let them run on the plastic because they could slip, fall, and hurt themselves.

Watering down the grass provides a similar surface, but because the grass will not be as slippery as the plastic, players should wear socks, long pants, and long shirts to avoid abrasions.

Another option is to have players practice sliding on a properly prepared infield. The infield should have a sandy or loose dirt surface and be smooth and firm, but not hard. It is a good idea for players to wear socks, long-sleeved shirts, and pants to help prevent sliding burns.

Baserunning Drills

(2.1) Leaving the Batter's Box Drill

Age: 9 years and up

Purpose: To train batters to focus their attention on first base and to run toward first base quickly

Equipment: Home plate and batter's box

Procedure: All players line up in back of the backstop or a safe distance from home plate. One player at a time stands in the batter's box and swings at an imaginary pitch. As soon as the swing is completed, the player turns and runs about 10 steps toward first base. (Do not let them run all the way to first base.)

Help your players through this drill by giving them one or two short instructions; say "Look at first base" or "Step toward first," rather than talking your players through the entire drill.

(2.2) Running Past First Base Drill

Age: All

Purpose: To teach players to run past first base

Equipment: Bases (one base for each group practicing the drill)

Procedure: Set up the bases at regulation distance. Line up players at home plate. Have your players stand in the batter's box, simulate a swing, and run past first base. Encourage them to run at game speed.

(2.3) Rounding First Base Drill

Age: 9 and up

Purpose: To teach players how to run around first base

Equipment: Bases (enough for each group practicing the drill)

Procedure: Set up bases at regulation distances and place a mark about 15 ft before first base so your players know where to begin to turn toward second base. Have your players get into position in the batter's box, swing, and run to and round first base. Players initially run at a moderate speed, then gradually increase their running speed as they become better at running around first base.

(2.4) Running from Home Plate to First Base Drill

Age: All

Purpose: To teach players to listen and react to the first base coach

Equipment: Three first bases, three home plates, one bat per player

Procedure: Set up three sets of home plates and first bases at regulation distances, and line up your players at home plate. This setup will let three players practice at the same time. The players swing a bat and run to first base. As the player approaches first base, the coach calls out, "Run past first" or "Round the base."

(2.5) Running the Bases Drill

Age: 9 years and up

Purpose: To give players practice running bases

Equipment: Infield bases

Procedure: Players start in the batter's box, simulate a swing, and run to first base. The coach at first base calls out, "Run through first base," "Take the turn," or "Run to second." After each runner has completed his or her turn, the next runner starts. Have base coaches at first and third bases direct your base runners. The third base coach directs runners reaching second base by calling, "Stay at second," "Round second," or "Run to third." Similar instructions are given when the runner reaches third base.

(2.6) Base Start Drill

Age: 9 years and up

Purpose: To practice running from one base to another base

Equipment: A complete infield set up with bases

Procedure: Set up an infield with bases and have one player act as the pitcher. Position base runners on first, second, and third bases. Have the base runners set up in the crouched position and run from the base just as the pitcher releases the ball. Rotate your players around the bases: New runners move to first base, and the runner on third base moves to the end of the line.

(2.7) Leaving Bases Drill

Age: 9 years and up

Purpose: To practice leaving the base as fast as possible and returning to base for tag-ups

Equipment: One complete set of bases

Procedure: Position players on first base, second base, and third base. Be sure each player assumes the correct starting position. Call out, "Go" or "Run" to start the runner toward the next base. Call out, "Leave," "Tag-up," or "Run" for leaving the base and tagging up after caught fly balls. Emphasize watching fly balls, listening to the base coach, and pushing off with the back foot. Rotate the runners around the bases: The runner on third base moves to the end of the line, and a new runner moves to first base.

(2.8) Lead-off, Running, and Steal Drill

Age: 10 and up

Purpose: To help players learn to lead off, steal, and run from one base to another. This drill is valuable for determining the distance each player can lead off a base.

Equipment: Bases and balls

Procedure: The drill proceeds through six stages. You can use each stage as a separate drill or all six stages to progressively teach and practice lead-off and baserunning components.

Stage 1: The ready position. Show your players the proper ready position and have them practice getting ready to lead off the base.

Stage 2: The sidestep. Show your players how to lead off using a sidestep motion and practice moving 20 ft to each side using the sidestep.

Stage 3: The turn and run or *the dive.* Show your players how to use the crossover step to quickly turn toward the next base or toward the base they occupy. When turning toward the next base, have them run a few steps. When turning toward the base they occupy, have them touch the base with the foot or dive and touch the base with the hand.

Stage 4: The lead-off. In this stage have your players determine how far they can lead off. For this you will need a pitcher and fielder. Have the runner take two lead-off steps and return to the base when the pitcher throws to the fielder. Each time your runner can return safely, have him or her lead off an extra half-step. The lead-off distance will be the distance prior to being thrown out.

Stage 5: Listen to the base coach. Use a base coach to instruct each player to "Lead off," Run," or "Return to the base."

Stage 6: The steal. Have base runners practice running to the next base as soon as the pitcher strides toward home plate. Have your pitchers vary the pitching motion so that your players learn to react in a game-like situation.

Part II: Defensive Play

Defensive baseball skills are much more specialized than are offensive skills. Hitting and baserunning are similar for all players regardless of whether they are first or sixth in the batting order. Defense is different because there are nine players on the field at once, and each player needs to learn the skills and responsibilities relative to his or her position.

Each chapter in the defensive section is devoted to the various defensive aspects of baseball. Separate chapters are included for (a) skills which all fielders need, (b) general infield and outfield skills, (c) infield and outfield skills specific to each position, (d) infield and outfield team play, and (e) pitching and catching.

Chapter 3: Defensive Fundamentals

Introduction: Defensive Skills

The physical skills needed to play defense vary according to the position played and the particular game situation. Conversely, each playing situation will determine the type of skills needed to make a play. Moving quickly to the ball and throwing hard are more powerful skills that do not require great precision. However, actually fielding or catching the ball and throwing accurately are more refined skills requiring greater precision; thus, beginning players may have difficulty performing more accurate and precise skills.

We recommend you begin by teaching your players defensive fundamentals and then progress to more advanced defensive concepts. If you follow this progression, your players will not only learn how to play defense, they will also understand the principles of defensive play. The following topics are described in this chapter to help you teach defensive fundamentals:

- Selecting, caring for, and using the glove
- Throwing mechanics
- Catching the ball
- General defensive drills

The Glove

Selecting the Glove

Selecting a baseball glove is important because it is the tool players use to field and catch, and without a well-fitting glove, defensive play will suffer. If you are able to talk to your players or their parents before gloves are purchased, point out two considerations: the size of the glove as compared to the size of the hand, and the size of the glove's pocket.

The glove should be small enough to fit comfortably on a player's hand, and the pocket should be large. Furthermore, the glove should be easy for the player to control. For young baseball players, a broken-in smaller glove will be much more useful than a larger glove. It is not a good idea for youngsters to play with an oversized glove in hopes of later growing into it (see Figure 3-1). Beginning players need a well-fitting glove from the outset in order to learn baseball skills. Oversized gloves that they cannot control will be an ineffective tool and will hinder skill development.

First, help your players decide which hand wears the glove. Most people can control the glove better with the nondominant hand and can throw better with the dominant hand. So, have your players hold up their throwing hand and place the glove on their nonthrowing hand.

Fig. 3-1

Caring for and Conditioning the Glove

Conditioning the glove will help your players control the glove and will improve their ability to field and to hold the ball. Conditioning is sometimes called *breaking in* the glove and will create a good pocket for the baseball by making it more manageable. Explain the following break-in procedures to your players:

1. Rub some hot water into the center of the glove and work it in.
2. Place two large balls such as softballs in the glove pocket and tie the glove around the balls as illustrated in Figure 3-2. This will help the glove form a large, rounded pocket.

Fig. 3-2

3. Leave the glove tied overnight; repeat this process each evening until the glove has formed a good round pocket and is very flexible.
4. Use glove oil, saddle soap, or leather oil periodically. Rub the oil into the glove and let the oil soak into the glove overnight. However, be sure to rub off any excess oil before you use the glove! The glove will gradually become strong and flexible.

Using the Glove

The hand should fit into the glove with all five fingers so that it becomes an extension of the catching hand (see Figure 3-3). Keeping all five fingers in the glove helps control the ball as well

Fig. 3-3

IMPROPER HAND PLACEMENT IN GLOVE

PROPER HAND PLACEMENT IN GLOVE

as protect the fingers. Demonstrate how the glove can be opened and closed as easily as moving the hand. Removing the index finger from the glove in order to increase pocket size is not a good idea. This actually reduces control of the glove and increases risk of injury to the exposed finger.

Throwing Mechanics

Because children grow up throwing rocks, balls, and flying discs, knowing how to throw is sometimes taken for granted. However, learning how to throw a baseball *accurately* takes much practice. The following discussion focuses on teaching your players the *overhand* throw. We suggest you wait until your players know how to throw overhand well before teaching the side-arm throw.

Two drills are presented at the end of this chapter to help your players practice throwing mechanics. The Flick the Ball Drill (3.1) focuses on the arm and wrist action, and the Throwing Action Drill (3.2) focuses on stepping into the throw and swinging the throwing arm.

The Grip

The way a player grips the ball will greatly affect how it is thrown; many throwing errors can be prevented if your players first know how to grip the ball properly. Explain to your players that the ball should rest only on the fingers and not in the palm (see Figure 3-4), with the thumb on the bottom of the ball and the index and second fingers spread on top. If the ball is held in the palm of the hand, it will be difficult to control. To help your players develop a firm but flexible throwing grip, have them practice the Ball Grip Drill (3.3).

Fig. 3-4

How to Throw

Although the mechanics of throwing can be very complex, they can and should be presented simply in these four easy-to-understand phases: the ready position, shifting onto the back foot, stepping toward the target and throwing the ball, and the follow-through.

Phase 1: Getting in the Ready Position
Have your players face the target squarely with the body evenly balanced on both feet, with a proper but comfortable grip, and with the eyes focused on the target, as shown in Figure 3-5. The importance of this preparation is to begin the throw, balanced and with the body and ball under control.

Fig. 3-5

Phase 2: Shifting
The body weight is simply shifted onto the throwing side (push-off) leg as the front foot is lifted off the ground. At the same time, the throwing arm swings back with the wrist cocked (see Figure 3-6).

Fig. 3-6

Phase 3: Throwing the Ball
The body weight should now shift onto the front leg as the back leg pushes forward. With this push, the front leg strides forward and lands slightly bent. This will help a player maintain balance and smoothly transfer energy from the push-off leg toward the target. You can really help your players by watching this phase carefully. If a player's stride is too long or too short, as shown in Figure 3-7, the throw will be inaccurate, and the stride should be adjusted.

Fig. 3-7

LONG STRIDE   SHORT STRIDE   PROPER LENGTH

After striding and planting the front foot, the upper body turns toward the target; this helps pull the throwing arm around the body (see Figure 3-8). After the arm moves forward, the wrist snaps to send the ball flying toward the target.

Fig. 3-8

Phase 4: Following Through
The follow-through is actually the result of a good throw because once the ball is released, a player can no longer affect the throw; therefore, a good throw will have a good follow-through. Demonstrate that in the follow-through, the throwing arm is extended and continues across the body. The leg used to push off (back leg) steps through and lands ahead of the glove-side foot (see Figure 3-9).

Fig. 3-9

Coaching Points for the Throw

1. Leg work is important because most of the power for the throw comes from the legs. To demonstrate, have your players try to throw without using the legs.
2. Insist players concentrate upon the target at all times, even during the follow-through.
3. The shoulders should remain level until the follow-through. If the shoulders are dipped up or down, the throw will be off target.
4. Snapping the wrist will put a backward spin on the ball; this indicates a good release and helps the ball travel in a straight line.

Quickness, Accuracy, and Speed

You will want your players to make quick, accurate, and fast throws. But the quicker the ball is released and the faster the ball is thrown, the more difficult it is to control. Because of this, it is more important for beginning players to first develop accuracy by throwing at moderate speeds, then gradually increase the speed of the throws while maintaining accuracy.

Teaching Progression for Throwing

Remember, your players will learn throwing best if they are taught in a purposeful progression.

Therefore, use the following progression to teach throwing to your players most effectively:

1. Introduce the grip.
2. Explain and demonstrate the starting position.
3. Teach players to shift the weight onto the back foot and prepare to throw.
4. Demonstrate and explain how to step toward the target and release the ball.
5. Teach players not to stop after the ball is released but to always follow through.
6. *Emphasize control.* Increase the speed of the throw while maintaining accuracy.

Catching the Ball

Catching a baseball involves excellent hand-eye coordination and much practice. Thrown balls travel a long distance and can often fool the fielder by changing direction and by giving the illusion of appearing to move faster as they approach. The Warm-up Catching and Throwing Drill (3.4) is very useful for developing the skills needed to catch a baseball.

Instructing Players to Catch

- Give the thrower a target by holding out the glove. This will help the thrower aim the ball (see Figure 3-10).

Fig. 3-10

PROVIDE A GOOD TARGET

- Move the body in line with the ball. Demonstrate how to step toward and away from the ball, and how to step sideways using a side-step motion as illustrated in Figure 3-11.

Fig. 3-11

MOVE TO THE BALL

- Watch the ball. Tell your players to look at the ball all the way from the thrower's hand into their glove.
- Catch the ball in the pocket of the glove, not in the fingers. Explain that the glove pocket is made to hold the ball while the fingers are made to give players control of the glove.
- Trap the ball with the throwing hand (see Figure 3-12). Let your players know that trapping the ball will help secure the catch and will allow them to grip and throw the ball more quickly.

Fig. 3-12

CATCH AND TRAP THE BALL

- Absorb the impact of the throw as shown in Figure 3-13, by allowing the glove to move toward the body after the catch. This is called *cushioning* the ball.

Fig. 3-13

CUSHION THE BALL

Your players will need to adjust the glove position depending upon the location of the throw. By using the guidelines listed below and as illustrated in Figures 3-14 to 3-17, instruct your players of the following body and glove adjustments:

1. If the ball is above the waist, have the fingers of the glove point up.
2. If the ball is below the waist, have the fingers of the glove point down.
3. If the ball is on the throwing side of the body, have the back of the glove face the body and the thumb face down.
4. If the ball is on the glove side of the body, instruct your players to hold the glove with the thumb up and the fingers pointing out.

Fig. 3-14

CATCHING ABOVE THE WAIST

Fig. 3-15

CATCHING BELOW THE WAIST

Fig. 3-16

CATCHING TO THE THROWING SIDE

Fig. 3-17

CATCHING TO THE GLOVE SIDE

Teaching Progression for Catching

1. Instruct your players on the proper use of the glove.
2. Stress the importance of concentrating on the throw.
3. Show your players how to move to the ball by stepping forward, backward, or to the side.

4. Explain that the ball should be caught in the pocket of the glove and trapped with the throwing hand.
5. Demonstrate how to cushion the catch by moving the glove toward the body.

General Defensive Drills

(3.1) Flick the Ball Drill

Age: 9 years and up

Purpose: To develop throwing skills by emphasizing strong wrist action and proper ball spin

Equipment: One ball for every two players, gloves

Procedure: Players work in pairs. Partners stand only 10-12 ft apart and face one another. Players flick the ball back and forth, using only the wrist and aiming at the chest. To isolate the wrist action from the arm motion, have the players bend and place their elbow in the palm of their other hand.

Fig. 3-18

(3.2) Throwing Action Drill

Age: All

Purpose: To help young players develop the proper arm throwing motion

Equipment: One ball for each player

Procedure: Have your players work individually. This drill is divided into two phases. In the first phase, have your players grip the ball properly. Then the players should practice getting into the ready position and shifting their feet, arms, and weight to prepare for the throw. In the second phase, have your players get set by shifting their feet, arms, and weight (end of the first phase) and complete the throwing motion by striding forward, pushing off the back leg, and swinging the throwing arm forward.

(3.3) Ball Grip Drill

Age: All

Purpose: To develop coordination of fingers and wrist for proper grip of the ball, and to develop strength in the fingers and forearm

Equipment: One ball for every two players

Procedure: Have players pair up. One player grips the ball with a proper throwing grip. The partner tries to remove the ball by moving it up and down and to the side. The player holding the ball should keep a flexible wrist and allow the hand to move up and down while maintaining a firm grip on the ball. The partner who is pulling on the ball should not jerk the ball, but should keep an even pull on the ball. After 30 seconds, players switch roles; this allows each player to rest his or her hand before the next repetition. Repeat this two to three times.

(3.4) Warm-up Catching and Throwing Drill

Age: All

Purpose: To loosen and warm up players prior to throwing hard

Equipment: Gloves and one ball for every two players

Procedure: Players pair up and throw to each other from relatively short distances. Players gradually increase the speed and distance they throw, but always throw comfortably, never hard.

Contest: Have players line up facing each other about 15 ft apart. Each time a pair successfully completes two throws apiece, each player takes one step back. Each time a ball is misthrown and not caught, each player takes one step toward the other.

Chapter 4: Fielding and Throwing Fundamentals

Introduction: The Importance of Judgment Skills

After your players have learned the fundamentals of throwing and catching, they will be ready to learn the fundamentals of fielding and throwing in game situations. They will learn to field balls hit on the ground and in the air; they will also learn to catch balls thrown from another part of the field while staying close to a base. Unless these fielding and throwing fundamentals specific to game situations are properly taught, your players will have difficulty playing team defense.

These skills involve the ability to visually judge the speed and distance of a hit or thrown ball. Thus, players must also learn how to react to the ball: Should they charge the ball or back up? Move to the right or left? Hold the glove up, down, or to the side? The abilities of visual judgment and movement reactions are not easy for beginning players to learn. As their coach, you will need to be patient and encourage them to develop these abilities. Keep this in mind as you teach your players the following information for fielding and throwing in game situations:

- The principal rule of fielding
- Developing good fielding and throwing habits
- Playing the ball and throwing
- The ready position
- Moving to the ball
- Taking in ground balls
- Taking in fly balls
- Throwing the ball
- Tagging runners out
- Fielding and throwing drills

The Principal Rule of Fielding

Before you teach these defensive skills, be sure your players understand the principal rule of fielding, which is: *Keep the ball in front*. By keeping the ball in front of the body, your players will eliminate many errors caused by reaching out to the side and not moving to the ball. This rule also directs the positioning of your outfielders, preventing fly balls from being hit beyond them.

Developing Good Fielding and Throwing Habits

The development of fielding and throwing fundamentals is extremely important for proficient game play now and enjoyment of the game in the future. The more your players practice to develop correct habits, the better they will play today and in the future.

Tell your players to think of habits as ways people act automatically without concentrating on what they are doing. For example, the way they eat and scratch their head are considered habits. Habits are learned by repeating an action so many times that you do not consciously decide what to do, you just act. You can help your beginning players develop correct playing habits by following the guidelines explained in the ACEP Level 1 book *Coaching Young Athletes* and by structuring practices in such a way that players repeatedly perform these fundamentals. As you do this, provide encouragement and correct mistakes positively through demonstrations and explanations.

Playing the Ball and Throwing

Fielding can be divided into two main categories: *playing the ball* and *throwing*. Explain that playing the ball means reacting to and catching a hit or thrown ball; throwing involves moving the ball from one part of the field to another in order to complete defensive plays.

In addition to teaching the *how's* of fielding and throwing, you will also need to teach the *why's* and *where's*, or playing strategy. For example, after the ball is taken in, where should it be thrown, and why should the players throw there? Many strategy factors such as the speed of the runners, their position on base, the number of outs, and the score of the game will determine where the ball is played. These playing strategy factors are discussed in the section on playing strategy in chapter 7.

The Ready Position

Once the game begins, every player must be ready to perform the responsibilities of his or her position. But, if the player is not in a comfortable ready position, he or she will not be able to move easily or play well. The best ready position depends upon the player. A ready position that is comfortable for one player may not be good for another. Therefore, as you teach the ready position, help each player find the style that is both comfortable and effective.

The Ready Position Stance

The ready position is quite simple. Players stand with the feet about hip-width apart, the knees bent, and the body weight over the balls of the feet, as illustrated in Figure 4-1. Gloves should be open wide and held comfortably inside the legs. Because ground balls can change direction or bounce unexpectedly, watching the ball all the way into the glove is very important. The Fielding Position Drill (4.1) is a good drill for practicing the fielding ready position and for preparing to move to the ball.

Fig. 4-1

Coaching Points for Ready Position

1. For a good base of support, stand with the feet about hip-width apart.
2. To move quickly in every direction, keep the knees bent.
3. For quick movement, keep the weight on the balls of the feet. Standing flat-footed slows movement to the ball.
4. Be sure the hands are held low between the legs with the glove open wide.

Moving to the Ball

Once the ready position is learned, you can teach your players how to react and move to the ball. It is important they learn to react to the ball as soon as it is hit. If they wait until the ball is halfway down the infield, they will not be able to reach it in time to make a play.

Determining Direction of Movement

Your fielders can reach the ball quickly by determining the direction of the ball and moving toward it; most often players need to move forward or backward and then change direction. Demonstrate how to move forward by stepping out of the starting position, running forward, and keeping the arms low to the field, as shown in Figure 4-2.

Fig. 4-2

The Side Step
The *side step* is one of the two methods used to move from side to side. Use the side step for mov-

ing short distances by shuffling the feet from side to side, but not crossing them. The advantage of the side step is in keeping a balanced stance while moving to the ball (see Figure 4-3).

Fig. 4-3

The Crossover Step
The second method, the *crossover step* illustrated in Figure 4-4, should be used when a player needs to turn and run quickly for longer distances. To teach the crossover step, have each player step across the body with one foot while the body pivots around the other foot that remains planted. After the foot has crossed over, the player is in position to run in that direction.

Fig. 4-4

CROSSOVER STEP

Moving Backward
When your players need to move backward, they can simply step backward or use the crossover step to turn to the side and then run back. For moving short distances, stepping back is more effective than crossing over and running back: For example, if a ball is popped up to the second baseman, he or she has plenty of time to watch the ball while taking a few steps backward.

The crossover step should be used to run a long distance quickly. For example, if the ball is hit over the head of the second baseman and toward the shallow outfield, the second baseman should use the crossover step to turn and run to the outfield.

Coaching Points for Moving to the Ball

1. Move to the ball when it is hit. Waiting for the ball will waste time and could prevent the team from making an out.
2. Watch the ball all the way into the glove.
3. Use the side step or crossover step to move sideways; use the crossover step or back step to move backward.

Taking in Ground Balls

The next step in learning to field is called *taking in* the ball and involves getting the ball up from the ground and into the glove. Have your players bend down with the legs (keeping the back straight) and reach out the glove to meet the ball (see Figure 4-5). Emphasize that trapping

Fig. 4-5

FIELDING POSITION

the ball with the throwing hand is as important as fielding a thrown ball. Practicing the Fielding Ground Balls Drill (4.2) and the Charge the Ball Drill (4.3) will reinforce these points and help your players develop the ability to field ground balls.

Cushioning the Ball
When taking in a ball, encourage your players to keep the wrists firm yet flexible in order to

cushion the ball. With a flexible wrist, the force of the ball should softly punch back the glove and prevent the ball from popping out.

Fielding Short Hops

Many ground balls will *short hop*, or bounce, from the ground directly in front of the fielder. These are the tricky and illusive grounders that are difficult to field. There is no guaranteed method for fielding short hops, but it will help if your fielders have relaxed arms and hold the glove open and out in front of the body. Short hops can bounce wildly, so your players should be ready to rise up or down or move the glove quickly.

Coaching Points for Fielding Ground Balls

1. Get into position before the ball is taken in. Once again, emphasize the importance of being prepared to field the ball.
2. Watch the ball.
3. Trap the ball.
4. Cushion the ball.

Teaching Progression for Fielding Ground Balls

1. Teach players the ready position.
2. Teach players how to move forward, backward, and to the side.
3. Teach players how to take in and trap ground balls.
4. Progress from easy to more difficult ground balls by slowly rolling grounders thrown from short distances, gradually increasing the speed and distance.

Taking in Fly Balls

Explain to your players that when a ground ball is fielded, the runner must be thrown out, but if a fly ball is caught, the batter is *automatically* out. The two basic glove positions for taking in fly balls are illustrated in Figure 4-6. For fly balls caught above the chest, show your players how

Fig. 4-6

FLY BALL ABOVE CHEST

FLY BALL BELOW CHEST

to hold the glove above the shoulders with the fingers pointing upward. For fly balls caught below the chest, use the *basket catch* by holding the glove about waist height with the pocket facing upward.

Trapping Fly Balls

As with fielding ground balls, remind your fielders to trap the ball. However, be careful how you teach this because trapping fly balls is different from trapping ground balls. Instruct your players to hold the free hand behind the glove to first support the glove and cushion the ball, and then to close the glove around the ball, as shown in Figure 4-7.

Fig. 4-7

Calling for Fly Balls

Because fly balls travel across several infield positions, more than one fielder may try for the catch. Also, if a player is watching the ball, he or she may not see other players who are also trying to field the fly ball. You can prevent many unnecessary collisions by teaching your players to yell "Mine!" or "I have it!" when the fly is at its highest point (peak), as shown in Figure 4-8, so the player with the best position can watch the ball drop and make the catch.

Fig. 4-8

Judging Fly Balls

Beginning players may find fielding fly balls difficult because of the speed of the ball and the distance it travels. Several different indicators will help your players determine how well a fly ball is hit. The first indicator is the sound of the bat contacting the ball: The stronger and the more solid the sound, the better the hit. The second indicator for judging fly balls is the speed of the ball as it leaves the bat: The faster the ball leaves the bat, the better the hit and the farther it will travel. The third indicator for judging fly balls is the angle of the ball: The steeper the angle, the higher the ball will fly (see Figure 4-9). If a ball leaves the bat fast and has a moderate angle, it will travel farther than a ball that is hit fast and has a steep or low angle.

Unfortunately, no easy method exists for teaching how to determine what a solid hit

Fig. 4-9

sounds like (especially if a metal bat is used) or to teach the speed of a ball leaving the bat or to teach judging the distance a ball will travel. These skills are best learned through experience and repetitive practice. The Judging Fly Balls Drill (4.4) and the other drills listed in chapter 6, "Playing the Outfield," have been designed to provide the repetitive practice needed to learn these skills.

Coaching Points for Taking In Fly Balls

1. Watch the ball.
2. Stand up from the ready position.
3. Move sideways and backwards, using the side step, crossover step, or back step.
4. Call for the ball when it is at its highest point.
5. When catching fly balls above the chest, hold the glove facing up and above the chest. When catching fly balls below the chest, hold the glove about waist height with the open pocket facing the ball.
6. Trap the ball by placing the free hand behind the glove and closing the glove around the ball.

Teaching Progression for Fielding Fly Balls

1. Teach the ready position.
2. Teach how to move to the ball.
3. Instruct your players to call for fly balls.
4. Teach how to trap fly balls.
5. Progress from easy to more difficult fly balls. Begin with easy lobs from short distances. Gradually increase the distance and height of the fly balls.

Throwing the Ball

Once a ball is fielded, it should be thrown to the appropriate base or player as quickly and accurately as possible. To get extra power on the throw and maintain accuracy, teach your players the three phases of the *skip and throw* and practice the Step and Throw Drill (4.5), the Throw and Step Back Drill (4.6), and the Throwing for Points Drill (4.7).

The Skip

The first phase of the skip and throw is a short skip, as shown in Figure 4-10, which provides extra momentum and power. Show your players how to skip by taking a short hop on the back (push-off) foot while the front foot moves forward and the arms are drawn back.

Fig. 4-10

The Throwing Motion

This second phase involves the entire body, not just the arms. After skipping, the back foot pushes the body forward and the front leg steps directly toward the target. This push and forward step provides the power to whip the arm around and throw the ball (see Figure 4-11).

The Follow-Through

Remind your players that the follow-through is the result of a good throw. In a proper follow-through, the body pivots around the front foot while the throwing hand continues to swing across the body (see Figure 4-12).

Fig. 4-11

Fig. 4-12

Coaching Points for Throwing the Ball

1. Grip the ball in the glove.
2. Skip on the back foot, push off, and step toward the target.
3. Focus on the target and swing the throwing arm forward.
4. Follow through.

Teaching Progression for Throwing the Ball

1. Teach the skip. Emphasize a short, low skip rather than a long, high skip.
2. Teach the step and throw motion. Stress the coordination of the legs, arms, and body.
3. Teach the follow-through, which is the result of a good throw.
4. Combine the skip, step, and throw. Emphasize smooth and coordinated movements and an accurate throw.
5. Gradually progress from throwing easy, over short distances to throwing harder, over longer distances.

Tagging Runners Out

Now that your players know how to catch and field balls, they need to learn how to tag out base runners. This is an important fielding duty; it is also a situation where both the fielder and runner could be injured, so safety should be stressed. Demonstrate how to tag out base runners by studying the position and techniques shown in Figures 4-13 to 4-15 and explain the following points to your players:

1. Get into position behind and to the side of the base.
2. Catch the ball off to the side of the base.
3. Lay the glove down between the base and the runner.
4. Move the glove away after the runner has been tagged out.

Fig. 4-13

Fig. 4-14

Fig. 4-15

The first priority of every fielder is to stop the ball, so if the throw is not on target, teach your players to move away from the base and catch the ball (see Figure 4.16). Regardless of whether the runner is or is not tagged out, the ball must be caught, or the runner will definitely be safe and will probably advance to another base.

Fig. 4-16

Coaching Points for Tagging the Runner

1. Position your fielders behind and to the side of the base.
2. Catch and hold onto the ball.
3. Lay the glove down between the base and the runner.
4. Move away from the runner.

Teaching Progression for Tagging the Runner

1. Teach how to stand behind and to the side of the base.
2. Teach how to move to the ball and catch the throw before reaching the base.
3. Lay the glove down between the base and the runner.
4. After the tag is made, move the glove away from the runner.

Fielding and Throwing Drills

The following drills have been designed to help your players learn the skills essential to baseball defense. We recommend you select the drills which you feel will best help your players develop their baseball skills; then modify the drills to meet the age and ability levels of your players.

(4.1) Fielding Position Drill

Age: 9 years and up
Purpose: To teach and refine the fielding ready position
Equipment: None
Procedure: Divide players among coaches (8 to 10 per coach). Instruct and demonstrate the fielding ready position and have your players line up in a semicircle. Call out, "Set," "Down," or "Up!" On each command, the players should get set to field by bending their legs and getting down (as if taking in a ball) or by straightening their legs and rising up to move quickly. Be sure to watch for poor mechanics and give positive, meaningful feedback to correct the skill.

(4.2) Fielding Ground Balls Drill

Age: 9 years and up
Purpose: To teach and refine the skill of fielding ground balls
Equipment: One ball for every two players, gloves
Procedure: Pair up players. Position players facing each other a moderate distance apart. Start with players rolling easy ground balls to each other. Older and more skilled players can stand farther apart and throw ground balls harder.

(4.3) Charge The Ball Drill

Age: 9 years and up
Purpose: To develop aggressive movement to a ground ball and to develop proper fielding fundamentals
Equipment: Several balls, gloves
Procedure: If there is more than one coach, divide the team into two groups of 6 to 8 players. The players from each group practice with one coach. Have your players form two lines and face each other, 30 to 40 ft apart. Be sure your players are far enough apart to avoid interfering with

each other. Have the players in the first line throw easy grounders to their partners. Instruct your fielding players to charge the ball rather than wait for the ball. Alternate fielders and throwers after 10 throws.

(4.4) Judging Fly Balls Drill

Age: 9 years and up

Purpose: To develop the visual judgment needed for responding to and catching fly balls

Equipment: Balls, gloves

Procedure: Divide your players up among your assistant coaches. Have your players stand facing you from about 20 ft away. Throw each player relatively easy fly balls. Vary the height, arc, and speed of the balls you throw. As your players become more experienced and are able to catch these fly balls, move them farther from you and increase the difficulty of the fly balls. You should eventually progress to conducting this drill batting balls from the same distances as in actual games.

(4.5) Step and Throw Drill

Age: 9 years and up

Purpose: To practice the skip and throw

Equipment: One ball for every two players

Procedure: Pair up your players and position them a moderate distance apart. Have each player throw using the skip and throw. The skip should be low and short, and the player should step into the throw. This drill can also be modified to practice throwing after fielding a ground ball or fly ball.

(4.6) Throw and Step Back Drill

Age: 9 years and up

Purpose: To help players practice and refine throwing skills

Equipment: One ball for every two players, gloves

Procedure: Pair up players. Have partners stand reasonably close to each other. Players throw the ball back and forth. Each time the ball is successfully thrown and caught, the player who threw the ball takes a step back. When the ball is not caught, the player takes a step forward. This drill can also be used as a competition-type drill between team members.

(4.7) Throwing for Points Drill

Age: 9 years and up

Purpose: To develop the ability to focus on a specific spot before throwing and to throw to that spot accurately

Equipment: One ball for every two players, gloves

Procedure: Players work in pairs. Have players stand 30-40 ft apart and face one another. Players earn points by throwing to specific spots on the partner's body. Scoring: chest = 5 points; hips = 3 points; arms and legs = 1 point; head = 1 point; away from the body = −1 point (subtract a point from the player's score). Have players hold the ball where they catch it so their partner can evaluate and correct the next throw. Suggested winning score is 50 points.

Chapter 5: Positional Infield Skills

Introduction: Infield Playing Areas

Because baseball is such a popular game, many beginning players know some of the basics such as where the bases are located and where the pitcher and catcher stand. However, before they can practice team defensive plays, they must learn the coverage areas and the responsibilities for the following six infield positions presented in this chapter:

- First baseman
- Second baseman
- Shortstop
- Third baseman
- Pitcher
- Catcher

Teaching positional responsibilities is important for two other reasons. First, if your fielders stray outside of the positional areas or do not fulfill the duties of their position, overall team defense will suffer. Studying this chapter carefully and teaching your players their responsibilities will contribute greatly to an effective team defense. The Infield Teamwork Drill (5.1), the Backing-up Drill (5.2), and the Individual Position Drill (5.3) will give your players the experience of playing infield positions.

Second, we highly recommend that all beginning baseball players learn several different positions (see Figure 5-1). Beginning baseball players

Fig. 5-1

should not specialize at one position too soon. Let each player experience several positions, and then based on expressed preference, players can specialize as they mature.

First Baseman

The first baseman's coverage area is not particularly large. It extends from midway between home plate and first base and over to about halfway between first and second base (see Figure 5-2). The importance of this position is not in the coverage area but rather in preventing runners from reaching the base safely. If a runner can be thrown out before reaching first base, a scoring opportunity is eliminated, and the entire team can concentrate on the next batter, rather than on the batter and a base runner.

To field this area, position your first baseman a few steps toward second base and slightly behind first base. From this position, the first baseman can perform the following duties quickly and easily:

- Catching and fielding balls hit to the first base area
- Making force-outs by touching first base or throwing to other fielders covering first base
- Holding runners on first base
- Throwing to second base for force-outs
- Backing up plays at home plate and second base
- Relaying throws from right field

Fig. 5-2

Plays at First Base

Beginning players need to be taught how to make force-outs at first base. Begin by defining a force-out (see chapter 11 of the Planning Guide), and then emphasize the following two points: (a) Force-outs are more common at first base than are tag-outs; and (b) a force-out is good if the ball is caught and any part of the body touches the base. The key, then, is to touch the base with the back foot and to stretch out several feet to catch the ball, as illustrated in Figure 5-3. Explain that by stretching out, the ball is caught sooner, and as long as the back foot touches the base, the force-out is good.

However, although this position is great for force-outs, it is not good for moving after poorly

Fig. 5-3

thrown balls. Teach your players to be alert and to know where the throw is going before they stretch out for the catch. Remember, the first baseman's main priority is to catch the ball, even if it means leaving the base.

Coaching Points for Plays at First Base

1. Touch the inside of first base.
2. Reach out to catch the ball.
3. Leave first base to catch poor throws.

Throwing to First Base

When the first baseman fields a hit ball and cannot touch first base before the runner, the second baseman or pitcher must cover first base. By tossing the ball underhand to other fielders covering first base (see Figure 5-4), the ball will reach the base in time to make the out and will be easier to catch than will an overhand throw.

Holding Runners on First Base

To hold runners on first base and to reduce the probability of steals, teach your players to stand

Fig. 5-4

with the push-off foot on the inside edge of the base and to hold out the glove ready for throws from the pitcher (see Figure 5-5). From this position the first baseman can catch throws to first base and can swing the glove back to tag runners. If the ball is pitched, show your players how to move away from the base and get set to field the ball, as illustrated in Figure 5-6.

Fig. 5-5

Fig. 5-6

Cutting Off Throws to Home Plate

The first baseman must be ready to move in front of home plate to cut off relay throws (see Figure 5-7). Line up the first baseman about 15 ft in front of home plate. Also, emphasize listening for the catcher calling out "Cut off," or "Come through."

Second Baseman

The second baseman covers a large area from about midway between first and second base, over to second base, and from behind the

Fig. 5-7

pitcher's area to the shallow portion of right and center fields (see Figure 5-8). Even though this is a lot of ground to cover, the second baseman is close to the two bases where most plays will be made: first base and second base. This means that the second baseman will not make many long throws, can play from a relatively deep position, and can perform the following duties:

- Fielding balls hit to the coverage area
- Throwing to second and first base for force-outs
- Tagging out runners moving from first to second base
- Making force-outs and tag-outs at second base
- Covering first base on bunts and whenever the first baseman fields the ball

Fig. 5-8

- Relaying throws from the outfield to the infield
- Backing up second base when the shortstop is making the play

Shortstop

The shortstop has a wide area to cover: from second base almost to third base and to the shallow outfield. The best starting position for shortstops (see Figure 5-9) is about halfway between third base and second base; however, the ability of each player will determine his or her exact position. Because the shortstop has a large area to cover and because throws to first base are long, those players who are more mobile and who can throw far will be able to play from a deeper position; those players who are less mobile or who cannot throw as far will need to play a bit more shallow. Keep these points in mind as you teach your players the following responsibilities for the shortstop:

- Fielding all balls hit to the coverage area
- Throwing to second and first base for force-outs
- Relaying and cutting off throws from the outfield
- Covering second base on bunt attempts or when balls are hit to the second baseman
- Backing up second base when the second baseman is making the play

Fig. 5-9

Third Baseman

The third baseman covers the infield area from about halfway down the third base line over to the shortstop position and back to the shallow part of left field (see Figure 5-10). This is not a large area to cover, but because it is far away from first and second base, the third baseman needs to have a good throwing arm. Most beginning players bat right-handed and tend to hit the ball to the shortstop or third base area, so it is very important to teach the third baseman to guard the third base foul line. If a ball is hit down the line and past third base, it will roll a long way before it is fielded, and the batter will probably run to second base.

Fig. 5-10

A good playing position for the third baseman is to be a few steps from the foul line and slightly behind third base. From this position, the third baseman can guard the line and perform the following duties:

- Throwing to first base for force-outs
- Making plays at third base
- Relaying and cutting off throws from the outfield
- Covering bunts hit to the third base side of the infield
- Backing up the shortstop

Pitcher

A common misconception about pitching is that the pitcher has few fielding responsibilities. This is not true. You will need to stress that the pitching position is not just for throwing the ball to the batter. The pitcher is another defensive player and has the following fielding duties:

- Backing up plays at home plate
- Covering first base when the first baseman is fielding a ball
- Holding runners on first base
- Backing up second and third base on throws from the outfield
- Fielding bunts
- Cutting off throws to home plate

The defensive coverage area for pitchers extends from the back and sides of the pitching circle up to the home plate area (see Figure 5-11). In fact, the pitching follow-through places the pitcher in the front of the pitching circle close to the batter. This means pitchers must be prepared to react quickly to field balls after completing the pitch.

Fig. 5-11

The pitcher must also back up home plate. When backing up home plate, position your pitchers about 10 ft in back of the plate, in line with the throw. From this position the pitcher can still move in to home plate when throws get by the catcher.

Holding Runners on First Base

Pitchers and baserunners play a constant guessing game: Baserunners want to lead off of a base but not so far that the pitcher will throw them out; pitchers want to concentrate on the batter but, if the base runner has too much of a lead, should try to throw the runner out. According to baseball rules, the pitcher's throwing motion must be directly to home plate or to a base. The best method for throwing to a base is to step back off the pitching rubber, as shown in Figure 5-12.

Fig. 5-12

Backing Up Home Plate

Backing up home plate is different from backing up other bases, because instead of being behind the player or base, the pitcher is in front of home plate. To back up home plate, position your pitchers about 10 ft in front of the plate, but not in line with the throw, as shown in Figure 5-13. From this position, the pitcher will not interfere with the throw and can still move in to home plate when throws get by the catcher.

Fig. 5-13

PITCHERS BACK-UP HOME PLATE

Catcher

Just as pitchers do more than pitch, catchers must do much more than catch pitches. The catcher's fielding area, illustrated in Figure 5-14, extends behind the plate to the backstop, along the first and third baselines, and in front of the plate about halfway to the pitcher's circle. In addition to catching pitches, catchers have the following duties:

- Protecting the plate by tagging out runners who attempt to score
- Fielding balls hit near or behind home plate
- Throwing to first, second, and third bases for tag-outs
- Backing up first base
- Fielding bunts

Fig. 5-14

Catching Pop-Ups

Pop-ups hit near and in back of home plate present unusual problems for catchers. Other fielders will not be in position to help make the catch, and the catching equipment makes locating, moving to, and fielding the ball difficult. Show your catchers how to (a) turn toward the location of the pitch, (b) remove the facemask, and (c) throw the mask away from the play, as shown in Figures 5-15 to 5-16. These skills can be practiced by performing the Pop-Ups for Catchers Drill (5.4).

Fig. 5-15

Pop-ups hit close to the backstop are also difficult for young catchers. Show your players how to turn and face the backstop, as illustrated in Figure 5-16, rather than keeping the back to the backstop. As with your other fielders, instruct your catchers always to catch the ball with two hands.

Fig. 5-16

Tagging Out Runners at Home Plate

Tagging out runners at home plate is an important skill for the catchers and is the last chance they have to prevent a run from scoring. They must also be careful, because according to the rules, the catcher may not interfere with the runner by blocking the plate unless the catcher is tagging out that runner. Interfering with the runner could result in the umpire awarding the runner home plate.

Demonstrate the proper position for tag-outs at home plate, shown in Figure 5-17, by positioning your players in front of and to the third-base side of home plate. From this position, they can

Fig. 5-17

catch the ball and make the tag without interfering with the runner. After your players understand how to position themselves and make the tag, have them practice the Tag Plays at Home Drill (5.5).

Backing Up First Base

Another important responsibility of the catcher is backing up first base. Because the catcher is positioned behind the batter, he or she is in an excellent position to see where the ball is hit, to follow the batter to first base, and to recover balls that get by the first baseman (see Figure 5-18).

Running back and forth between home plate and first base is also a good way to wear out your players and eliminate volunteers for the catching position. We suggest you teach backing up first base to those players who are mature enough to handle this physical activity. Also, use more than one catcher each game.

Fig. 5-18

CATCHERS BACK-UP FIRST BASE

Dropped Third Strikes

An unusual play in baseball is **running on a dropped third strike**. Here is how it works: When no runner is on first base, with less than two outs, and the catcher drops a third strike pitch (with two outs first base can be occupied), the batter can run to first base. But, if the catcher can tag the batter or throw to first base before the batter/runner touches the base, the runner is out. The best way to handle a dropped third strike is for you to call out, "Dropped third strike" and let the catcher tag the runner or throw the ball. A good drill to practice throwing to first base on dropped third strikes is the Throwing From the Stance Drill (5.6).

Fortunately, these plays do not happen regularly. Several of the rule modifications found in chapter 12 of the Baseball Planning Guide eliminate the possibility of dropped third strike plays for players who may not be skilled or experienced enough to make these plays. We suggest you read and consider using these modifications. They can make playing baseball less confusing and more enjoyable.

Infield Play Drills

Several drills are presented to help your players develop their infield positional skills. We recommend you select the drills that you feel will most effectively benefit your players, then modify the drills to meet the skill level of your players.

(5.1) Infield Teamwork Drill

Age: 9 years and up

Purpose: To teach and refine players' abilities to work together on infield plays

Equipment: One set of bases

Procedure: You will need to instruct and to demonstrate the positional skills and responsibilities to your players. As your players take their infield positions, set up play situations with various outs and baserunning combinations. Hit or throw to different areas of the infield. Your players should field the ball and react by (a) backing up plays,

(b) fielding the ball, and (c) completing the play. This drill should be uncomplicated for younger and less experienced players. Older and more experienced players will be able to think through and execute more complicated plays.

(5.2) Backing-Up Drill

Age: 6 years and up

Purpose: To practice backing up other fielders

Equipment: One set of bases

Procedure: Position the fielders in the infield and outfield. You can use a reduced field for this drill by placing the bases 30 ft apart. Call out a fielding situation and throw a ball to begin the action. Have your players move to field the ball, complete the play, and back up other fielders.

(5.3) Individual Position Drill

Age: 9 years and up

Purpose: To provide players with an opportunity to work on skills specific to their defensive positions

Equipment: Gloves, balls

Procedure: Players report to their defensive positions and perform the following skills specific to their position:

Catchers practice

- shifting on low pitches in the dirt,
- catching stance and throws to all bases,
- fielding bunts and pop flies,
- catching cut-offs and throwing relays, and
- tagging runners out.

Pitchers practice

- covering first base,
- starting double plays,
- bunt coverage, and
- cut-offs from the outfield.

First basemen practice

- shifting around the bag,
- receiving various types of throws,
- starting double plays,
- bunt coverage,
- catching cut-offs and throwing relays, and
- throwing to pitchers covering first.

Second basemen and *shortstops* practice

- starting and finishing double plays,
- catching cut-offs and throwing relays,
- fielding slow rollers, and
- fielding all types of ground balls.

Third basemen practice

- moving to the right and left,
- slow rollers,
- catching cut-offs and throwing relays,
- bunt coverage, and
- starting double plays.

Outfielders practice

- judging and fielding fly balls, and
- fielding ground balls and throwing to the cut-off players.

(5.4) Pop-Ups for Catchers Drill

Age: 9 years and up

Purpose: To give catchers practice on pop-ups

Equipment: Catching equipment, bat, baseballs

Procedure: Hit or throw pop-ups to catchers in full gear. Give constructive feedback to the catcher's fielding attempts.

(5.5) Tag Plays at Home Drill

Age Group: 9 years and up

Purpose: To teach catchers the proper method of tagging out runners who are attempting to score

Equipment: Catching equipment, home plate

Procedure: The catcher wears full gear and assumes a position by home plate as if receiving a throw. The catcher's left foot should be placed on the front edge of the base so that runners can see the back half of the base. Have runners slide into home plate. Other fielders or a coach should throw the ball, timed barely to beat the runner, to the catcher. The catcher then tries to tag out the runner. Rotate catchers after 10 throws. Initially, have your catchers practice this drill without runners. The runners can be added after catchers become more skilled in executing tags at home plate.

(5.6) Catchers Throwing From the Stance Drill

Age Group: 9 years and up

Purpose: To teach catchers how to throw to second base

Equipment: Home plate, second base, ball, gloves, catcher's gear

Procedure: Set up bases and position players. Catchers should wear gear for this drill, even though the ball should be pitched slow. Catchers should receive pitches and throw to the bases. Rotate catchers and reposition fielders after 10 throws.

Chapter 6: Playing the Outfield

Introduction: The Last Line of Defense

Outfielders are an important part of your team's overall defense. They cover the largest area of the playing field and are the last players between the infield and the seemingly endless reaches of the outfield. Consequently, every ball hit to the outfield is a potential *big play* for the offense; therefore, outfielders must be alert and must communicate well with each other. Also, outfielders are valuable back-up players for the infield.

The following outfield responsibilities and topics for good defensive play are covered in this chapter:

- Positioning outfielders
- Outfield ready position
- Catching fly balls
- Fielding outfield grounders
- Throwing to the infield
- Communicating in the outfield
- Backing up plays
- Outfield play drills

Positioning Outfielders

Explain that the game of baseball requires three outfielders: The one positioned in right field is called the *right fielder*; another positioned in center field is called the *center fielder*; and the third positioned in left field is called the *left fielder*.

Position your outfielders as shown in Figure 6-1 so they can see the entire infield, including the pitcher, catcher, and batter. The better they can see all players on the field, the better they will be able to play the position. In general, position left fielders between the shortstop and third baseman, center fielders slightly to the left or right side of the pitcher, and right fielders between the second baseman and first baseman.

Fig. 6-1

Explain to your players that there is no predetermined method for playing these positions. The exact positioning of your outfielders will depend on several factors: (a) the strength of the hitter, (b) the game situation, and (c) the condition of the playing field. For example, position your out-fielders deeper in the outfield for strong hitters and closer to the infield for weak hitters. Outfield positioning will also vary if the batter is right- or left-handed. Explain that left-handed hitters tend to hit toward right field; therefore, the outfielders should shift toward right field when there is a left-handed hitter (see Figure 6-2).

Fig. 6-2

Outfield Ready Position

The ready position for outfielders is similar to the ready position for infielders, the difference being that outfielders should not bend down. Instruct your outfielders to stand upright keeping the knees flexed, arms relaxed, and the weight balanced on the balls of their feet, as illustrated in Figure 6-3. If players bend down too much, or stand flat-footed, they will get into the ready position before moving to the ball. Getting into a good ready position will allow outfielders to react quickly.

Catching Fly Balls

Fundamentals for catching fly balls have been covered in chapters 4 and 5. Only those factors which pertain particularly to outfielders are discussed here.

Fig. 6-3

Instruct your outfielders to be alert and always ready to make a play. The sooner they are in position and ready to play, the sooner they will be able to make any adjustments necessary to catch the ball. Consequently, if they do not hustle, they could be out of position and will not be able to field balls. A good drill to practice setting up in the ready position, moving to the ball, and catching fly balls is the Fielding Fly Ball Drill (6.1).

Playing alertly and hustling are also important points for you as a coach. Lazy players can cause others to play in the same manner, just as highly motivated players can influence other players to hustle; therefore, set an example: Be enthusiastic and show some hustle yourself. Praise those players who hustle and encourage them to praise each other.

Judging Fly Balls

Judging the flight of fly balls is a difficult skill to teach beginning baseball players. Traveling farther than expected and curving across the field, fly balls can be deceiving. There is no easy way to learn how to judge fly balls. Some guides for judging fly balls were presented in chapter 4. The best way to learn this skill, however, is through practice and experience.

Several uncontrollable factors can affect field-ing fly balls. Explain to your outfielders that they need to be aware of how the wind can affect the flight of a fly ball and how to avoid being blinded by the sun.

Playing in the Wind

A strong wind can be particularly annoying for beginning players, so remind them to check the speed and direction of the wind each inning (see Figure 6-4). Explain that a fly ball will tend to follow the direction of the wind. If the wind is blowing from home plate to the outfield, the ball will travel farther, so your players should play slightly deeper than usual. If the wind is blowing from the outfield toward home plate, the ball will stall out, so your players should play slightly closer to the infield.

Fig. 6-4

Because the wind can blow the ball around, remind your players that catching fly balls is easier running forward than backward. Therefore, whether they play deeper or closer than usual, the ball should not get beyond them. Remember the principal rule of fielding: *Keep the ball in front.*

To emphasize these points, try out the following exercise: Have your players run forward about 50 ft and catch a fly ball at the end of the run. Then have them run backward and catch a fly ball. Your players will soon realize the importance of keeping the ball in front.

Sunlight

Bright sunlight can also disturb outfielders, making easy plays quite difficult. By holding up the glove to shade the eyes, as shown in Figure 6-5, outfielders can block out the sun and be ready to reach out and catch fly balls. However, be sure

Fig. 6-5

your players know not to block out both the sun and the ball; they still need to watch the ball until it is caught.

By now your players should be able to tell you that using two hands is the best way to catch a ball (see Figure 6-6) because (a) it helps secure the catch, and (b) it sets up the throw by gripping the ball while it is in the glove. Even so, it is a long way to the outfield fence, and you may need to remind them to use two hands every time they catch a ball.

Fig. 6-6

When Fly Balls Fall in Front of a Player

No matter how fast a player can run, some balls will still fall in front of them. The best method for catching such low balls is to use a *basket catch*, holding out the glove about waist height with the palms facing up (see Figure 6-7). To

Fig. 6-7

secure the ball in the glove, show your players how to bring the glove with both hands in to the body, as shown in Figure 6-8.

Because the basket catch is often used to catch balls on the run, it is a difficult skill for beginning players. Wait until your players are able to run and catch well before teaching the basket catch; then use the Basket Catch Drill (6.2) to practice this skill.

Fig. 6-8

BRING GLOVE INTO THE BODY

Fielding Outfield Grounders

As mentioned earlier, the outfield is a large area to cover, and each ball not fielded correctly greatly helps the offensive team. Because of this, it is important for outfielders to field ground balls cleanly, to throw to the infield quickly, and to hold runners to as few bases as possible. The best method for blocking, fielding, and throwing ground balls in the outfield is called the *blocking position*. To teach the blocking position, follow Figure 6-9, and show your players how to

Fig. 6-9

(a) move to the ball, (b) bend down on the glove-side knee, and (c) place the glove between the legs.

After fielding, the ball can be thrown back to the infield in a continuous motion. Follow the illustration in Figure 6-10 to show your players how to stand up and step into the throw. Use the Outfield Ground Ball, Fly Ball Drill (6.3) to practice fielding and throwing hits to the outfield.

Fig. 6-10

Throwing to the Infield

Where to Throw the Ball

Once the ball is fielded, it needs to be thrown with an overhand throw to the infield. Throwing sidearm will cause the ball to curve slightly, making it inaccurate and difficult to catch; but an overhand throw will ensure a straight and more accurate throw (see Figure 6-11).

Also, throw so that the ball gets into the infield quickly. The fastest way to get the ball to the infield is to use a *relay* (explained in chapter 7, "Team Defense") with several low, straight throws, rather than one long, high-arching throw. High throws go a long distance but also

Fig. 6-11

Fig. 6-12

PLAYERS CAN COMMUNICATE BEFORE . . .

. . . OR AFTER

take more time, thus allowing a runner to reach another base. Long, high throws also place great stress on the arm and shoulder and after several throws could make the arm sore.

Communicating in the Outfield

It is essential to teach teamwork and communication among players at this level. Not only will overall team play improve, but your players will also learn social skills such as listening and cooperating with others. Also, communicating effectively does not just happen; it is a technique which requires repeated practice using drills such as the Outfield Teamwork Drill (6.4).

Instead of speaking in long, detailed sentences, teach your players to use short statements or one word signals such as "Mine" or "Relay to short-stop" (see Figure 6-12). Long sentences take too much time and confuse players, whereas short statements transmit accurate information quickly, thus enhancing performance.

Backing Up Plays

Even when your outfielders are not making a play, they can contribute to the overall performance of the team by backing up other fielders, especially the outfielder next to them, as shown

Fig. 6-13

in Figure 6-13. Backing up can also be hazardous if not done correctly, and safety should be a primary concern for you as a coach.

Assignments for Backing Up the Infield

To ensure safety and enhance outfield team-work, follow the suggested back-up assignments for outfielders listed below (see Figure 6-14):

- Right fielders back up plays at first base and back up the second baseman.
- Center fielders back up plays at second base and back up the second baseman and short-stop.
- Left fielders back up plays at third base and back up the third baseman.

Fig. 6-14

Back-up Positioning

Now that your players know which fielders to back up, they will need to be shown how to position themselves to back up other fielders. Moving about 20 ft behind the backed-up fielder or base, as shown in Figure 6-15, will provide enough distance between both players to catch passed balls. If positioned too closely, back-up players will have trouble seeing passed balls and may not have enough time to react.

Fig. 6-15

20 FEET

Outfield Play Drills

(6.1) Fielding Fly Balls Drill

Age: 9 and up

Purpose: To develop and to refine the skills needed to run after and catch fly balls

Equipment: Balls, gloves

Procedure: Line up the fielders in an open grass field or outfield area. The player at the front of the line moves from the other players to a position where he or she can catch fly balls you hit or throw. Have the fielder throw the ball back to you while the next player moves into position. Be sure to hit or throw the balls in different directions with various speeds and arches.

(6.2) Basket Catch Drill

Age: 9 and up

Purpose: To develop the skills needed to catch a fly ball on the run using a basket catch

Equipment: Balls, gloves

Procedure: Have the players line up about 50 ft from the coach. The coach should be at a right angle to the players. Instruct your players to run across the field as you throw easy fly balls straight ahead and to catch these flys using the basket catch. (The right angle enables you to see how well your players are able to perform the basket catch.) We recommend that you begin throwing low, easy fly balls to the players. As your players improve in this skill, you can adjust the height and difficulty of the fly balls. The importance of throwing balls straight ahead is that the players, positioned 50 ft away, will have to run to reach and catch the ball.

Fig. 6-16

(6.3) Outfield Ground Ball, Fly Ball Drill

Age: 9 and up

Purpose: To work on outfielding fundamentals

Equipment: Balls, gloves, bats

Procedure: Position your players throughout the outfield and hit various fly balls and ground balls for them to field. Encourage your players to move to the ball quickly instead of waiting for the ball.

(6.4) Outfield Teamwork Drill

Age: 12 and up

Purpose: To teach outfielders to work together

Equipment: Balls, gloves, bat, bases

Procedure: Place one set of outfielders in defensive positions, and place extra outfielders in the infield to receive throws. Tell them that an imaginary runner is on base. The outfielder who will play the ball is not told where the runner is. As the outfielder turns away, the coach signals the location of the runner, the number of outs, and the score. (More than one runner can be on base.) Hit balls to the outfielders from behind second base, and have the outfielder closest to the fielder catching the ball call where to throw the ball.

Chapter 7: Team Defense

Introduction: Working Together

The previous chapters described how to perform, teach, and practice individual baseball skills. You will be coaching a baseball team, however, so part of your job as a coach will be to teach your players team defensive situations. Baseball truly is a team sport, and few plays can be accomplished by players working alone. Working together as a team requires cooperation with other players and a willingness to follow the directions you provide. For many players, this may be their first experience playing on a team, and the manner in which you teach teamwork and cooperation will have a lasting effect on their attitude about team sports. We strongly recommend that you teach teamwork using a positive approach, considering the needs of the players on your team rather than the outcome of the game. For if your players perform their skills well and work as a team, the winning or losing will take care of itself.

This chapter will help you teach and practice team defensive skills by presenting the following topics:

- Defensive playing strategies
- Force-outs
- Bunt coverage
- Fly ball coverage
- Steal coverage
- Relays
- Cut-offs
- Double plays
- Team defensive drills

Familiarize yourself with these defensive topics and introduce them to your players in the order presented. Your players will not benefit much from double-play practice unless they are able to field and throw to second base and to first base effectively. Consider the skill level and playing experience of your players when introducing them to team defensive plays. Challenge your players with new skills, but proceed slowly and deliberately, taking into account their abilities and experiences.

Defensive Playing Strategies

It will be helpful to your players if you introduce playing strategies by reviewing the objectives of the offensive and of the defensive teams. They should learn that the offensive team tries to hit the ball, to run the bases, and to score runs; in contrast, the defensive team tries to prevent the offensive team from hitting, from running the bases, and from scoring runs by "putting out" that team.

Explain that the defensive team uses certain playing *strategies* to make outs and to control the offensive team. These strategies can become quite complicated and confusing for beginning players.

Instead of teaching beginning players several specific plays for specific situations, we recommend you teach a few general rules that govern defensive playing strategy. Once your athletes understand the general rules of defensive playing strategy, they will be able to apply these rules to specific situations.

Fig. 7-1

"Strategies? Where should I throw the ball?"

Introducing your players to baseball game strategy need not be time-consuming nor a distraction from practicing fundamental skills. In fact, practice is the best time to learn strategy. By using the Playing Strategy Drill (7.1) during practices, you can teach your players baseball skills and baseball strategy.

Rule 1: Hold the Runner

The first rule of baseball strategy is to keep each base runner from advancing to the next base (see Figure 7-2). This rule is in effect each time a pitch is thrown or a play is made. Of course, the best way to hold a runner is to put out the batter before he or she reaches first base. Stress that holding the runner is the most important rule to follow.

Fig. 7-2

RULE 1: HOLD RUNNERS AT A BASE

Rule 2: Throw Ahead of the Runner

Demonstrate how throwing ahead of the runner helps to put out the runner or prevent the run-

ner from advancing, as shown in Figure 7-3. Stress that Rule 2 and Rule 1 work together in helping control the offensive team.

Fig. 7-3

RULE 2: THROW AHEAD OF RUNNER

Rule 3: Throw to a Central Position

Sometimes players will not be able to throw ahead of a runner but can still throw to a central position such as second base or the pitcher in order to prevent runners from advancing. For example, if a ball is hit to the outfield, and a runner on second base runs to third base, the best play would be to throw the ball to the third baseman, second baseman, or to the pitcher (see Figure 7-4)

Fig. 7-4

RULE 3: THROW TO A CENTRAL POSITION

Rule 4: Make the Sure Out

The fourth rule of baseball playing strategy is to get the sure out. It is better to make a sure out than to try for an out players are not certain they can make, even if a runner moves to another base or scores a run. For example, when runners are at first base and third base, and a ball is hit to the shortstop, as presented in Figure 7-5, the run at home plate would be difficult to make, so the out should be made at second base.

Fig. 7-5

RULE 4: MAKE THE SURE OUT

Rule 5: Make More Than One Out

Try to make more than one out each play is the final rule of baseball defensive strategy (see Figure 7-6). However, making more than one out is the least important of all the defensive strategy rules and should be followed only after a sure out is made. This is especially true when players bobble or mishandle a ball. When this occurs, they should make the first *sure* out before attempting to make a more difficult out as part of a double play.

Fig. 7-6

RULE 5: MAKE MORE THAN ONE OUT

Your players will understand Rule 5 better as you explain *double plays*. Double plays can be made when (a) a fly ball is caught for an out and is thrown back to a base to force out a runner; or (b) the second baseman or shortstop fields a ball and touches second base to force out a

runner, then throws to first base to force out the batter. The most common double plays involve the second baseman and shortstop working together. This strategy is explained in detail later in this chapter.

Teaching Progression for Baseball Strategies

1. Teach Rule 1. This will help your players understand the objectives of defensive play.
2. Teach Rules 2 and 3. These rules will help your players understand where to throw the ball to best accomplish their defensive objectives.
3. Teach Rule 4. Rule 4 establishes the priority for making outs. Always encourage your players to make the sure out.
4. Teach Rule 5. This is the least important of all defensive strategies for beginning baseball players. Teach this rule after your players have demonstrated the ability to make multiple plays.
5. Practice making plays based upon these rules in game situations.

Force-Outs

Force-outs, if explained correctly, should not be difficult for beginning players to understand. Simply explain that a force-out is when a defensive player catches a ball and touches a base before the runner does. (See chapter 11 in the Planning Guide for a more complete description of force-outs.) To become proficient at making force-outs, players must learn the positional assignments described in chapter 5, and they must learn how to receive throws from other players by practicing the Force-out Practice Drill (7.2). As a general guideline, force-outs are made by the fielder responsible for that base. You can help your players understand their force-out assignments by demonstrating the following situations:

Situation	Player Responsible
1. Force-out at first base	First baseman
2. Force-out at second base	Second baseman
3. Force-out at third base	Third baseman
4. Force-out at home plate	Catcher

Sometimes a ball is hit so that the fielder responsible for the force-out fields the ball. When this happens, the following two plays are possible: First, the fielder responsible for the force-out fields the ball and also makes the out. However, this should be done only if the ball is hit close to the base as shown in Figure 7-7. Second, the player closest to the base fields the ball and throws to the player responsible for backing up that base. These coverage responsibilities are as follows:

Fig. 7-7

Situation	Player Responsible
1. Force-out at first base when the first baseman fields the ball	Pitcher or second baseman
2. Force-out at second base when the second baseman fields the ball	Shortstop
3. Force-out at third base when the third baseman fields the ball	Pitcher or shortstop
4. Force-out at home plate when the catcher fields the ball	Pitcher

Coaching Points for Force-Outs

1. Have the players cover the bases.
2. Be sure players are ready to back up other bases.
3. First priority is to catch the ball, then touch the base.

Teaching Progression for Force-outs

1. Teach how to move to the base and receive the throw.
2. Teach how to back up a base and receive the throw.
3. Begin with easy throws and with players walking through their assignments on shortened base paths.
4. Gradually progress to using balls thrown at regular speeds; then have players run through their assignments on a regulation field.
5. Practice making force-outs in game situations.

Bunt Coverage

Fielding softly hit balls, called *bunts*, is one of the most difficult plays in baseball. Because bunts do not roll far, the base runner has more time to reach the base, and the infielders must run in to the ball, leaving bases uncovered. Throws to the bases are often hurried and inaccurate, so outfielders must run in to back up the infield.

Assigning specific responsibilities to each infielder will help your players know exactly how to play bunts and will help to eliminate confusion among players. Consequently, practicing bunt coverage using a drill such as the Bunt Reaction Drill 7.3 is essential for developing a solid defense.

Player Positions

The positioning of your players will depend upon their fielding area and where the ball is bunted. As shown in Figure 7-8, bunts are usually placed

Fig. 7-8

Pitchers and catchers also have fielding responsibilities in bunt situations (see Figure 7-10). Pitchers cover the area directly in front of the pitching circle, and catchers cover the area immediately in front of home plate.

Fig. 7-10

between home plate and the pitching circle and along the foul lines. Therefore, your players will need to move toward these areas when a bunt is anticipated.

The difficulty of fielding bunts is increased when they are hit along the foul lines. Players must then decide whether the ball will remain in *fair territory* or will roll into *foul territory*. If it is clear that a ball will roll foul, teach your players not to touch it until after it rolls foul. This will place a strike on the batter, reducing the probability of other bunt attempts. *Beware*, however. Bunts that roll close to the foul line can be deceiving. As a general rule, if the ball is close to the foul line but not rolling foul, field the ball and try for the sure out.

When you notice a bunt situation, move the third baseman and first baseman into the shallow infield where they can charge bunts (see Figure 7-9). By staying close to the foul line, they can judge whether the ball will stay fair or roll foul.

Because the first baseman and third baseman move in, the shortstop and second baseman must cover all three bases. When there is no runner on second base, have the shortstop move over to second base, and the second baseman move over to first base, as shown in Figure 7-11.

Fig. 7-11

When a runner is on second base, the object of the defense is to prevent the runner from moving to third base. In this situation, the shortstop covers third base rather than second base, as illustrated in Figure 7-12.

Fig. 7-9

Fig. 7-12

Fielding the Bunt

More than one player may be able to field a bunt, so to avoid confusion, a priority system should be used. This priority system depends upon where the ball is bunted and upon who reaches the ball first. When a bunt is hit to a player's coverage area, that player has priority for fielding the bunt. However, the best priority system is to teach the player who reaches the ball first to call out "Mine," as shown in Figure 7-13, and for the other fielders to leave the ball alone.

Fig. 7-13

CALL FOR BUNT, FIELD,
AND THROW FOR THE OUT

Coaching Points for Fielding Bunts

1. Demonstrate the responsibilities and coverage areas for each position.
2. Demonstrate the back-up responsibilities of the second baseman and shortstop.
3. Encourage your players to field the ball properly and to throw accurately.

Teaching Progression for Fielding Bunts

1. Teach your players their responsibilities, coverage areas, and back-up responsibilities.
2. Walk the players through fielding bunts and throwing to bases.
3. Gradually progress to fielding bunts and throwing to bases at regular speeds.
4. Practice fielding bunts in game situations.

Fly Ball Coverage

Fly balls travel across several positions, so more than one player may be able to field a fly. In other situations, fly balls hit to one area may be played easier by another fielder. To eliminate any confusion concerning which players field fly balls, your team will need to use a priority system similar to the one used for fielding bunts. This system is shown in Figures 7-14 to 7-19 and explained below:

1. When fly balls are hit to left center field or right center field, center fielders have priority over other outfielders.

Fig. 7-14

CENTER FIELDERS HAVE PRIORITY
OVER OTHER OUTFIELDERS

2. Because it is easier to catch a ball while running forward than running backward, outfielders have priority over infielders.

Fig. 7-15

OUTFIELDERS HAVE PRIORITY
OVER INFIELDERS

3. Because pitchers and catchers are usually not in a good position to field infield fly balls, the other infielders have priority over pitchers and catchers.

Fig. 7-16

OTHER INFIELDERS HAVE PRIORITY
OVER PITCHERS AND CATCHERS

4. The second baseman and shortstop will have a better angle to see and to field fly balls hit behind first base and third base than will the first baseman and third baseman. When fly balls are hit behind first or third base, the second baseman and shortstop have priority.

5. Catchers have priority for pop-ups which are near or behind home plate.

Fig. 7-17

FOR HITS BEHIND FIRST OR
THIRD BASE SHORTSTOPS OR
SECOND BASEMEN HAVE PRIORITY

Fig. 7-18

CATCHERS HAVE PRIORITY FOR
BALLS HIT NEAR HOME PLATE.

6. Because the pitcher's follow-through makes it difficult to move and to field fly balls, pitchers should call for pop-ups only when necessary.

Fig. 7-19

PITCHING FOLLOW-THROUGH
MAKES IT DIFFICULT TO REACT QUICKLY

Coaching Points for Fly Ball Coverage

1. Teach players to watch the ball.
2. Teach players to call for the ball.
3. Teach players to know their fielding areas and responsibilities.

Teaching Progression for Fly Ball Coverage

1. Teach positional coverage areas.
2. Practice catching easy fly balls thrown from short distances.
3. Progress to calling for and catching more difficult fly balls on a regulation outfield.
4. Practice fly ball coverage in game situations.

Steal Coverage

Explain that *stealing a base* is an attempt by a runner to run to another base and the ball has not yet been hit or a batter walked. Because the base runner is not forced to that base, he or she must be tagged out, not forced out. Instruct your fielders to do two things when a base runner tries to steal: (a) move to the base and (b) call out "Steal!" (see Figure 7-20).

Fig. 7-20

Steal

The Throw

The distance between home plate and second base makes throwing to second base particularly difficult for beginning catchers; but it is the base most often stolen. Always play it safe! Teach catchers not to throw unless they are sure they can throw the runner out. The best way to throw from the crouched position is to step into the throw just as outfielders throw from the blocking position. Stress for low, accurate throws. You cannot risk having the ball get by the fielder, allowing the runner to advance to another base.

Backing Up

There is always the possibility that throws will get by the fielder, so every fielder has back-up responsibilities. The shortstop backs up second base; the third baseman covers third base; the first baseman backs up home plate; outfielders move in; and the pitcher should be ready to back up the next possible play.

Coaching Points for Steal Coverage

1. Position players slightly behind and to the side of the base.
2. Emphasize watching the ball, making the catch, and tagging the runner.
3. Other players should move into the back-up positions.

Teaching Progression for Steal Coverage

1. Teach the coverage areas and back-up positions.
2. Demonstrate how to bend down, place the glove in the path of the runner, and move away after the tag is made.
3. Practice covering steal attempts by walking through steal situations on shortened base paths.
4. Gradually progress to practicing steal coverage at regular speed on regulation base paths.
5. Practice steal coverage in game situations.

Relays

When a ball is hit to the outfield, the best method for throwing it back to the infield is to use a *relay* in which several players work together. Relaying the ball is quite simple for beginning players to learn. Have them move into the shallow outfield, receive the throw, and throw the ball to the infield (see Figure 7-21).

Fig. 7-21

Relaying to Home Plate

More than one relay player may be needed when balls are hit deep to the outfield and thrown to home plate. In these situations, players who are free of responsibilities move into position and become additional relay players.

Coaching Points for Relay Throws

1. Be sure all fielders move into relay and back-up positions.
2. Emphasize accurate throws and sure catches.
3. Encourage relay players to throw using the hop step.

Teaching Progression for Relay Throws

1. Begin practicing relay throws from moderate distances with easy throws.
2. Gradually increase the distance and speed of the relay throws.
3. Practice relay throws in competitive situations.

Cut-Offs

Sometimes a throw will need to be caught, or *cut off*, before it reaches its target. For example, if it is obvious a runner will score before a throw reaches the catcher, the ball should be cut off in front of home plate (see Figure 7-22). Cutting off a throw could also help throw out runners who are trying to take extra bases. Two drills which are especially useful for practicing cut-offs are the Cut-Off and Relay Drill (7.4) and the Team Throwing for Points Drill (7.5).

Fig. 7-22

Position cut-off players about 10 ft ahead of the base where the play is to be made. Most often, throws will be cut off at third base and home plate. For throws to third base, the shortstop should be the cut-off, and for throws to home plate the pitcher should be the cut-off.

The third baseman and the catcher can help the cut-off players by calling out "Come through" when the ball should not be cut off, or by calling "Cut off" when the ball should be cut off (see Figure 7-23). Other players may become excited and want to help by calling out, but discourage this. The third baseman and catcher are the only players who know if the play can be made and are the only players who should make the call.

Coaching Points for Cut-offs

1. Emphasize accurate throws and catches.
2. Emphasize moving into position before the ball arrives.

Fig. 7-23

"Cut-off"

3. Teach your fielders to practice calling "Come through" and "Cut off."
4. Emphasize making the tag-out properly when the ball does come through.

Teaching Progression for Cut-offs

1. Explain the purpose of cut-offs to your players.
2. Demonstrate the proper cut-off positions.
3. Demonstrate the proper cut-off calls, "Come through" and "Cut off."
4. Practice cut-offs from short distances with easy throws.
5. Gradually progress to practicing cut-offs from regulation distances with throws at regular speed.
6. Practice cut-offs in game situations.

Double Plays

Remind your players that *double play* is the term used for making two outs in one play. The most common double play is when the shortstop and the second baseman work together to complete a force-out at second base and then throw to first base to force out the batter. Of course, this can only happen if (a) a runner is on first base, and (b) a hit forces the runner to second base, as illustrated in Figure 7-24. Several useful drills for teaching and practicing double plays are the Receiving Tosses Drill (7.6), the Ground Balls into Double Play Drill (7.7), the Double Play Practice Drill (7.8), and the Double Play Practice with Runner Drill (7.9).

Fig. 7-24

Covering Second Base

Explain that the second baseman and shortstop work together to cover second base. The second baseman covers the base when the ball is fielded by the shortstop or the third baseman. The shortstop covers the base when the ball is fielded by the second baseman or first baseman. If the pitcher fields the ball, the player with the best position should move to second base.

Making the Double Play

Learning how to make double plays will be enjoyable if you teach each component in its proper sequence, as illustrated in Figures 7-25 to 7-27. First, teach your players to toss the ball so it is caught before the fielder reaches the base. Second, after catching the ball, teach your players to touch and step away from the base. The final part of this sequence is to throw to first base accurately.

Fig. 7-25

Coaching Points for Double Plays

1. Shortstops cover second base if the ball is fielded on the first base side of the field; sec-

Fig. 7-26

Fig. 7-27

ond basemen cover second base if the ball is fielded on the third base side of the field.

2. Toss the ball underhand, so the fielder catches it before reaching the base.

3. Touch second base for the first out, step away from the base, and throw to first for the second out.

Teaching Progression for Double Plays

1. Begin by having infielders practice throwing from second base to first base.

2. Practice tossing to the player covering second base.

3. Practice receiving the toss, touching and stepping away from second base, and throwing to first base.

4. Practice with bases close together, and then practice from the regulation distance.

5. Practice double plays in game situations.

Team Defense Drills

In addition to the drills referenced in this chapter, the Three-Player Drill (7.10), the Reduced Playing Field Drill (7.11), the Game Situation Drill (7.12), the Infield and Outfield Drill (7.13), and the Practice Game Drill (7.14) will help your players practice working together as a defensive unit. Feel free to modify these drills when necessary to better aid your coaching and the skill development of your baseball players. The Planning Guide section of this book provides realistic application of these drills for skill development and for team practice leading up to the first game.

(7.1) Playing Strategy Drill

Age: 9 years and up

Purpose: To introduce and to explain playing strategies to your players

Equipment: None

Procedures: To maximize your practice time, divide your players among your coaches. Place your players at each position on the field and present Playing Strategy Rules 1 through 4 (pp. 68-69) by setting up specific playing situations. Explain how these rules would specify where the ball should be thrown and why these rules apply. Introduce the rules in a progressive manner, and practice several situations for each rule before moving to the next rule.

(7.2) Force-out Practice Drill

Age: 9 years and up

Purpose: To teach and practice making force-outs at each base

Equipment: Gloves, balls, bases

Procedure: Introduce and explain force-outs to your players. Divide your players among your coaches to maximize your practice time. Set up situations where force-outs would occur at first base, second base, third base, and home plate. Throw or hit ground balls and fly balls to your players and have them throw for the force-out. It is important that you help your beginning players learn where to throw for force-outs by presenting them with specific situations and by explaining where to throw for the force-out.

(7.3) Bunt Reaction Drill

Age: 9 years and up

Purpose: To develop skills required for playing the bunt

Equipment: Balls, bats, gloves

Procedure: Divide your team in half: Have one half work with one coach while the other half works with another coach. If there is only one coach, have your players double up on positions and take turns fielding. Place your fielders in their infield positions (including pitcher and catcher). The pitcher will pitch to the batter (coach), who squares to bunt. The coach may also simulate bunt situations by indicating the number of outs, number of runners on base, and the bases that the runners occupy. When the ball is bunted, instruct your players to charge and field the ball, to move to the proper bases, and to back up other positions. Be sure to bunt the ball in all directions of the infield. Have players switch positions after the ball has been bunted three times in each direction (third base line, first base line, and straight ahead).

(7.4) Cut-off and Relay Drill

Age: 9 years and up

Purpose: To develop relay-throwing skills

Equipment: Balls, gloves

Procedure: Players work in groups of five. Arrange your players in a straight line with each player 60 to 70 ft apart. Beginning players should be positioned closer than more experienced players. Have the first player throw to the second player, who throws to the third player. Once the last player in line catches the ball, the process starts again in the opposite direction.

(7.5) Team Throwing for Points Drill

Age: 12 years and up

Purpose: To develop throwing accuracy

Equipment: Gloves, baseballs, infield set-up

Procedure: Assign a player to each position on the field. Teach your players the number of their position (as indicated in the numbering system of an official scorebook: pitcher-1, catcher-2, first baseman-3, second baseman-4, third baseman-5, shortstop-6, left fielder-7, center fielder-8, right fielder-9). Have the pitcher begin the drill by executing a skip and throw to the player whose number you call out. Because beginning players may have difficulty remembering the number of their fielding position, call out the name of the player or the position that fielder is playing.

(7.6) Receiving Tosses Drill

Age Group: 9 years and up

Purpose: To practice receiving tosses near second base and making tosses from different areas using shortstop and second base positions

Equipment: Ball, base, gloves

Procedure: The shortstop gets in position near second base and receives tosses from the second baseman, who practices making throws from different areas of that position. Following 10 to 15 tosses, the second baseman stays near second base and receives throws from the shortstop.

(7.7) Ground Ball into Double Play Drill

Age: 12 years and up

Purpose: To provide practice for performing double plays

Equipment: First and second base, gloves, ball

Procedure: Have one player stand near the pitcher's mound and throw a variety of ground balls and short hops to the shortstop and second baseman. Let both infielders practice fielding, tossing the ball to start the double play, and executing the necessary pivot and throw to first base.

(7.8) Double Play Practice Drill

Age: 9 years and up

Purpose: To introduce, to teach, and to practice double plays

Equipment: Three bases, gloves, balls, bat

Procedure: Place first and second base half their usual distance apart. The shortstop, second baseman, and first baseman stand in their usual positions in relation to the bases. Toss ground balls to the shortstop, who fields and throws to the second baseman, who throws to first base to complete the double play.

(7.9) Double Play Practice with Runner Drill

Age: 12 years and up

Purpose: To practice double plays in a gamelike situation and to give players practice running

Equipment: Infield set-up, balls, bat, gloves, helmets

Procedure: Third basemen, shortstops, second basemen, first basemen, catchers, and pitchers are positioned in the infield. All other players are runners and should wear helmets. One runner starts at first base, and one runner starts in the batter's box. As you hit ground balls to the infielders, the runner at home plate runs to first, and the runner on first base runs to second base. Instruct the runners to run off to the side of the bases to avoid running into the fielders or into the throw. After each play, the runner at first base remains at first base and prepares to run to second base. The other runner moves from the bases and waits his or her turn to run from home plate again.

(7.10) Three-Player Drill

Age: 9 years and up

Purpose: To practice all the fundamentals of fielding, throwing, and catching

Equipment: Balls (one for every three players), gloves

Procedure: Arrange the players in a triangle, with players 30 to 40 ft apart. One player rolls various types of ground balls and fly balls to the other two players. Ground balls should vary from fast ground balls and short hops to slow rollers (depending on the age group and skill level).

(7.11) Reduced Playing Field Drill

Age: 9 years and up

Purpose: To explain specifics of baseball in a modified setting

Equipment: Three bases, home plate, balls, and gloves

Procedure: Set up an infield with bases only 30

ft apart. Have some players take their positions on the field, while other players remain at home plate to be runners. Throw or hit balls to the infielders, who field and throw to complete plays. Rotate players after five throws to each position.

(7.12) Game Situation Drill

Age: 9 years and up

Purpose: To provide players with an opportunity to work on skills specific to their defensive positions

Equipment: None necessary, but can use gloves

Procedure: Position your players at their defensive positions and set up game situations by putting runners on base and calling the number of outs. After each simulation, have your players get into the ready position, imagine another type of game situation, and execute the play. This can be a fun drill for your players, especially if you let your players set up their own game situations.

(7.13) Infield and Outfield Drill

Age: 9 years and up

Purpose: To practice effective pregame defense, or pregame warm-up

Equipment: Complete field, balls, gloves, bat, catcher's equipment

Procedure: Have your players assume their defensive positions You can design any situation you wish your team to practice. The following is an example of how you could use this drill:

- *Outfield Phase.* Hit two fly balls and two ground balls to each outfielder. Instruct the outfielders to throw to the infielders as though they were in a real game. Hit several balls to each position.
- *Infield Phase.* Hit several balls to each infielder. The infielders should throw to first base, second base, or third base. Coaches can call out where to throw the ball.
- *Double-Play Phase.* The procedure continues as described above, but now the infielders practice double plays.
- *Throw Home Phase.* Hit a final ground ball to each infielder. Instruct the infielder to field the ball and to throw to the catcher at home plate.

After catching the ball, the catcher rolls the ball back to the infielder, who charges the ball and throws to first base, then runs off the field.

- *Completion Phase.* The coach concludes the drill by hitting a pop-up and bunt to the catcher.

7.14 Practice Game Drill

Age: All

Purpose: To practice baseball skills in a game setting

Equipment: Balls, complete infield set up, bats, helmets

Procedure: Divide the team in half by selecting two teams of equal ability. Play a game following the rules of your league or organization. Allow each player the opportunity to practice playing two positions. Do not end an inning with 3 outs. Instead, end each inning after each offensive player has batted, even if there are less or more than 3 outs.

Chapter 8: Pitching

Introduction: An Essential Defensive Skill

Ask your players to imagine a baseball game without pitching. There would be no hitting, fielding, or baserunning. In short, without pitching (with the exception of T-ball) baseball would not be much fun. But, pitching is also an important defensive skill. The more effective the pitcher, the less chance of batters reaching base and less chance of their scoring runs. Also, pitching is a difficult skill to learn well. The combination of strength and endurance, of timing, accuracy, and control are essential for the development of pitching skills in beginning baseball players.

The following topics are presented in this chapter to help you teach pitching fundamentals:

- The youth league baseball pitcher
- Care and conditioning of beginning pitchers
- Analyzing the pitching delivery
- Pick-off Moves
- Pitching Drills

The Youth League Baseball Pitcher

Let every player interested in pitching have an opportunity to learn pitching skills. Not every player will be interested, and not all pitchers will be able to pitch in all games; however, every player should be given the opportunity to learn pitching skills. Remember that maturational rates vary among children of similar age. Children who are large, fast, and strong for their age may be later surpassed by children who are shorter, slower, and not as strong at an earlier age. Allowing every player to learn pitching skills will be like planting seeds: Some will grow well this season, and others will grow better in the future. The important point is that each player has the opportunity to learn and to develop this skill.

Consequently, do not channel your players into certain positions based upon how strong, fast, and large they are at a certain age. Encouraging beginning players to experience and to learn skills for all playing positions will not only add to their immediate enjoyment, but will also allow them to adjust and to play positions more suited to their abilities later in life.

Care and Conditioning of Pitchers

Pitching is a skill that places much physical stress on the pitching arm, the back and the legs. Explain that the legs are used to provide most of the power for the pitch, therefore, the legs must be kept strong and flexible. Similarly, the back provides a base of support for the legs and arms and helps turn the body so the throwing arm can swing around to release the ball. The throwing arm and shoulder act like a whip to pull the arm around the body and snap the ball toward home plate.

To emphasize these points try the following three exercises: First, have your players try throwing without using the legs and notice the loss of speed and power. Second, have them try to throw keeping the back straight, and see how the loss of flexibility hurts the throw. Third, have your players try to throw without bending the elbows or wrists and notice the lack of control.

Keep these body parts strong and flexible by following the conditioning guidelines and exercises presented in this chapter and by studying and employing the training principles presented in the sport physiology and sport medicine chapters of the ACEP Level 1 book, *Coaching Young Athletes*.

Guideline 1: Warm-Up and Cool-Down

Pitchers must warm up properly by slowly exercising the legs, arms, and back before pitching so that the body is ready to play hard. If they do not take the time to warm up properly, they can become sore and risk prolonged injury. After pitching they should cool down by letting the body slowly stop exercising. If they stop throwing all at once, without gradually slowing down, they could develop sore arms. If your pitchers remain in a game at another position, the activity of playing that position could serve as a cool-down, but if they come out of a game, be sure they cool down with another player.

The following exercises are recommended for warming up and cooling down your pitchers:

- Hold the arms out to the side and swing them in a circular motion, as shown in Figure 8-1.

Fig. 8-1

- Swing the arms around the shoulders in a windmill fashion, as shown in Figure 8-2.

Fig. 8-2

- Simulate a throwing motion without a ball.
- Jogging.
- Easy throwing with a ball, gradually progressing to throwing harder (for the warm-up). Reverse this procedure for the cool-down.

Guideline 2: Develop Muscular Strength and Endurance

Pitching a ball fast many times requires a combination of muscular strength and endurance that can be developed by performing an exercise many times using a moderate resistance. If the resistance or weight used is too light, your pitchers will develop more endurance than strength and will be able to pitch for a long time but not have much power. If the resistance or weight is too heavy, they will develop more strength than endurance and may be able to pitch fast, but not for very long.

Several exercises for developing muscular strength and endurance are provided for you. These exercises stress using one's own body weight as the resistance or using a partner for help, thus eliminating the equipment and facilities that are not available to your players. Be sure your players can perform at least two sets of 10 repetitions without becoming overly tired. As the season progresses, gradually increase the number of repetitions for exercises that use one's own body weight as resistance. For exercises that do not use body weight as resistance, gradually increase the number of repetitions and the resistance.

- *Running.* Have your pitchers begin running once or twice around the field during practice. Gradually increase this distance throughout the season.
- *Striding leg presses* or *mountain climbers.* Stride out in front of the body; lower and raise the body using the legs. Switch legs and repeat. (see Figure 8-3).

Fig. 8-3

- *Toe raises.* Stand with the legs comfortably apart and raise up and down on the balls of the feet, as illustrated in Figure 8-4. As players become stronger, have them exercise one foot at a time.

Fig. 8-4

- *Hip twists.* Spread the legs hip-width apart and twist the body from side to side (see Figure 8-5).
- *Partner towel pull.* One player holds a towel, rope, or shirt and pulls in a throwing motion while a partner applies resistance throughout the throwing motion, as illustrated in Figure 8-6.
- General exercises: push-ups, half sit-ups (see Figure 8-7), and jumping jacks.

It is important that you recognize the abilities and limitations of beginning players, especially

Fig. 8-5

Fig. 8-6

Fig. 8-7

45°

the pitchers. Be patient and teach them pitching skills accurately. It would not be prudent to overwork children who are well coordinated and physically mature for their age and risk long-term injury to bones and muscles. Remember, these are young athletes. There will be plenty of time to develop skills as they grow physically and gain playing experience.

The Selection of Young Pitchers

It would also not be prudent to neglect players of lesser ability and maturation by denying them the opportunity to try pitching. We encourage you to allow all your players to try pitching and decide for themselves whether or not they want to concentrate on this position.

You must keep in mind that young people who are late maturers often surpass those who are early maturers in size, strength, and ability. To neglect a young player lacking physical maturity may be detrimental to their future skill development and playing ability.

Analyzing the Pitching Delivery

Because of differences in physical development and throwing styles, each pitcher will use a slightly different pitching delivery. Teach the following phases of the pitching motion, allowing your players to develop their own style. If their style clearly interferes with the skill, you can take steps to adjust the way they pitch.

The five phases of the pitch are the (a) stance, (b) wind-up, (c) push-off and back swing, (d) forward arm swing and release, and (e) follow-through. Demonstrate and teach each pitching component as part of a smooth, continuous motion, using these phases as coaching guides. The stance, wind-up, and push-off and back swing phases should be relatively slow, whereas the release and follow-through phases should be faster and explosive. Have your pitchers practice the Tarp Target Drill (8.1) and the Hit the Mitt Drill (8.2) to practice these five phases.

The Stance

Explain that the stance is the position of the pitcher on the pitching rubber. According to baseball rules, the pitcher can set up in several different positions, but the two most common stances are the *stretch* position and the *wind-up* position. Whatever stance your players use, at least one foot must be in contact with the pitching rubber.

The Stretch Position

For the stretch position the pitcher stands in front of the pitching rubber with the push-off foot

Fig. 8-8

touching the front edge and the striding foot comfortably in front of the body (see Figure 8-8).

The advantage of the stretch position is that the pitcher can easily step back off the rubber and throw to a base. Following the illustration in Figure 8-9, show your players how they can step back off the rubber and throw to first base, or step toward first base.

Fig. 8-9

The Wind-Up Position

Explain that the wind-up position is used to pitch the ball with more speed and power than the stretch position. However, it is more difficult to step and throw to a base from the wind-up position than from the stretch position. Thus, coach your players to use the wind-up when a runner need not be held close to a base or when first base is not occupied.

As shown in Figure 8-10, the wind-up position begins with the pitcher standing on the rubber

Fig. 8-10

facing home plate. Only one foot must touch the rubber so the other foot can be on, ahead of, or behind the pitching rubber.

The Wind-Up

Teach the *wind-up* by having players grip the ball and keep the throwing hand in the glove until the arm is swung forward, preventing the offensive team from seeing what type of pitch will be thrown. Although this point may not seem applicable to beginning players who throw only one pitch, it is a skill that should be taught while your players are learning to pitch.

From the Stretch Position
The wind-up from the stretch position is very short (see Figure 8-11). The striding foot is raised off the ground, the weight shifts onto the push-off leg, and the arms move back.

Fig. 8-11

From the Wind-Up Position
Figure 8-12 demonstrates how the wind-up begins by shifting the body weight onto the foot

Fig. 8-12

behind the rubber while the hands come apart and swing backward. Then, the body weight shifts to the push-off leg, the arms swing forward, hands come together in the glove, and the body pivots on the push-off foot so that the glove-side shoulder points toward home plate.

The remaining phases of the pitching delivery are very similar whether your players pitch from the wind-up position or the stretch position. The wind-up and the stretch positions will not be presented separately for these remaining phases, but you will need to show your players how to execute each phase properly for each position.

Push-Off and Back Arm Swing

Following Figure 8-13, demonstrate how the throwing arm reaches back as the weight shifts forward and the front foot strides out. This push forward generates much of the power for the pitch; it should be powerful, but controlled.

Fig. 8-13

Forward Arm Swing and Release

So far the pitcher has been moving the arms and body to provide power, but the most important part of the pitching motion is the release, which channels all this power into an accurate and controlled pitch. Many players think the release involves only the arm and wrist, but it also involves the forward stride and foot plant, which direct the throw.

The Stride

Explain that the length of the pitching stride greatly effects the release of the pitch (see Figure 8-14). If the stride is too short, the power developed by the legs will not be transferred to the back and arms; as a result, the pitch will be slower and less accurate.

Fig. 8-14

A stride that is too long can cause the pitch to be released late and lowers the body. This reduces the power transferred to the back and arms and disrupts the pitching motion. Consequently, a long stride causes pitches to be slower and more erratic.

Because every pitcher will have slightly different deliveries, there is no specific distance for the pitching stride. Rather than teaching pitchers to stride a specific distance, help them determine an appropriate stride length by watching pitching form and the flight of the ball. If the pitch is inaccurate, lacking speed and control, adjust the pitching stride. Once pitchers can throw well from a comfortable position, make another mark where the stride foot lands and have them try to step to that spot each pitch.

Foot Placement

Another factor affecting the pitching release is the placement of the striding foot (see Figure 8-15). Explain that the pitch will follow the direction of the striding foot. If the foot is placed off to the side, the pitch will be off to the side. The best foot plant is directly toward home plate.

Fig. 8-15

Poor foot placement can be corrected several ways. First, draw a line from the pitching rubber toward home plate and have pitchers practice stepping straight ahead onto the line. Although this is a direct solution, it may interfere with your pitcher's natural motion. If this occurs, use the second method: Have pitchers adjust the position on the pitching rubber. For example, if a pitcher throws off to the left, have that pitcher stand further to the right on the pitching rubber. The third method is to combine striding straight ahead and adjusting the position on the pitching rubber.

The Arm and Wrist

The action of the arm and wrist are the final contributors to the pitching release. Demonstrate how the arm swings around the body and the

Fig. 8-16

wrist snaps, releasing the ball from the fingers. We recommend teaching your players to pitch using an overhand arm motion (see Figure 8-16), which is more accurate and places less stress on the arm than does the sidearm motion.

The Follow-Through

As with all throws, a good pitching follow-through results from a proper pitch; no amount of arm waving or body twisting can change the pitch. The better the pitch, the better the follow-through. Following Figure 8-17, show your players how the throwing arm continues to swing downward and across the body, while the body pivots around the striding foot, and the push-off foot moves slightly in front of the body. From this follow-through position, the pitcher can get ready to field quickly.

Fig. 8-17

Coaching Points for the Pitching Delivery

1. Establish the pitch by using the appropriate stance.
2. Concentrate on pitching to the target.
3. Shift the body weight onto the push-off foot and turn the glove-side shoulder toward home plate.
4. Push forward, stride toward home plate, and reach back with the throwing arm.
5. Swing the throwing arm forward.
6. Snap the wrist.
7. Follow through.

Teaching Progression for the Pitching Delivery

1. Teach the stretch and wind-up stances.
2. Teach the wind-up for both stances.
3. Teach the push-off and back arm swing.
4. Combine the stance, wind-up, and push-off phases.
5. Teach the forward arm swing and release.
6. Teach the follow-through.
7. Combine all of these phases into a continuous, flowing movement.

Pick-Off Moves

After your pitchers are able to throw accurately and effectively, you can teach them how to throw over to a base to pick off base runners. The three guidelines that follow will help your players understand when to pick off base runners. Study these guidelines and take the time to explain them to your players. Knowing when to throw and when not to throw to a base will reduce unnecessary errors and will increase your pitcher's effectiveness. Use the Pick-off Move Drill (8.3) to practice throwing to bases.

However, when your pitchers try to throw out base runners or pitch to batters, they must be careful not to *balk*, or fake a pitch. Umpires determine balks by watching the movement of the pitcher toward home plate. If the pitcher begins to throw to home plate and then throws to a base, a balk will be called.

Guidelines for Picking Off Base Runners

1: Lead with the striding foot. According to baseball rules, pitchers must throw in the direction they step with the striding foot. For example, if your pitcher initially steps toward first base, the throw must go to first base. Similarly, if your pitcher steps toward home plate, the pitch must go to the batter.

2: Hold the base runner by stepping off the pitching rubber (see Figure 8-18). By stepping back off the rubber, the pitcher can throw to a base or hold the ball. Runners will not try stealing if the pitcher steps off the rubber, and the pitcher will not balk.

Fig. 8-18

3: Pitchers are not required to throw to second or third base. Whether your pitchers make a move to second base or third base while standing on the rubber or stepping off the rubber, they are not required to throw the ball. This means a pitcher in the wind-up position can fake a throw to second base or third base, and not worry about being called for a balk. It also means that pitchers can use the wind-up position whenever no runner is on first base, or when base runners are on first base and second base, because in these two situations, there is no need to keep the runner close to first base.

Pitching Drills

The following drills have been designed to develop the skills needed to pitch accurately and consistently. We urge you to modify these drills to the ages and skill levels of your players.

(8.1) Tarp Target Drill

Age Group: 9 years and up

Purpose: To help pitchers develop pitching control and accuracy

Equipment: Tarp, net or backstop with strike zone target area marked

Procedure: Have pitchers practice delivering pitches to various spots on the tarp. Pitch from a close distance, then from the regulation pitching distance after they have developed a good pitching motion and ball release.

(8.2) Hit the Mitt Drill

Age Group: 9 years and up

Purpose: To develop a pitcher's ability to throw at specific targets

Equipment: Catching gear, balls

Procedure: Pitchers and catchers get into position at a regulation distance from one another with catchers behind home plate. Have catchers give the pitcher a target by positioning the catching mitt at various positions around home plate. After your pitchers have developed adequate accuracy and control, add batters to this drill.

(8.3) Pick-Off Move Drill

Age: 12 years and up

Purpose: To practice throwing out runners on the bases

Equipment: Complete infield setup, 3 balls, helmets

Procedure: Position the pitcher on the pitching rubber, the fielders on the bases, and a runner at each base. Pitchers practice throwing to first base, second base, and third base. Most pick-off throws will be to first base. Therefore, emphasize throwing to first base more than to second base or third base. Base runners practice leading off and returning to the base. Fielders practice moving to the bases, catching the ball, and making the tag.

Chapter 9: Catching Pitches

Introduction: A Challenging Position

Catching is a difficult and challenging position for beginning players: They must wear protective equipment too large in relation to their physical size; they must see and catch balls while looking through a mask; they must move quickly to field balls with a heavy, oversized mitt; and they must squat behind the plate for long periods of time. Even so, catching is a very important position. The catcher receives all pitches, throws to the bases, and is the last defensive player to prevent runs from scoring. Another vital aspect of catching is helping the pitcher in any way possible. This includes (a) warming up the pitcher before games, (b) helping detect problems in the pitcher's delivery, and (c) helping pitchers maintain their confidence.

The fielding responsibilities of catchers were covered in chapter 5, "Positional Infield Skills." Presented in this chapter are the duties of the catcher as a member of the *battery*, or duo of the pitcher and catcher; included are the following topics:

- Catching stances
- Receiving pitches
- Blocking pitches
- Catching drills

Catching Stances

Squatting Stance

The first stance, shown in Figure 9-1, is a squatting position with the feet about hip-width apart and the glove-side (back) foot slightly behind the throwing-side (front) foot. To get into this position, have your players stand with the feet spread apart, the toe of the back foot even with the heel of the front foot; then simply squat down. With the feet spread apart and in the front-to-back position, it is easy to remain balanced, to shift to block pitches, and to step and throw. However, this position places stress on the upper legs, causing catchers to become sore and tired.

Fig. 9-1

CATCHER'S SQUATTING STANCE

Kneeling Stance

The second position is a kneeling position that eliminates much of the stress from the upper legs, but does not provide as much mobility for the catcher. As illustrated in Figure 9-2, the glove-side knee rests on the ground slightly behind the throwing-side foot and is very much like the outfield-blocking position.

Fig. 9-2

CATCHER'S KNEELING STANCE

Neither catching stance is a natural position and there is a trade-off between comfort and mobility. To take advantage of the mobility offered by the squatting stance and the comfort of the kneeling stance, have your players alternate between these positions. When the pitcher is getting set, and the catcher presents a target, use the kneeling stance; then to catch pitches, shift into the squatting stance.

Coaching Points for the Catcher's Stance

1. Position catcher directly behind home plate.
2. The feet should be about hip-width apart.
3. Keep the legs in a front-to-back position.
4. Balance the body weight between both legs.
5. Keep the back straight and the rear down.

Receiving Pitches

To receive pitches, the catcher needs to be set before the pitch is thrown. Demonstrate how to set up holding the mitt in a fingers-up position and present a steady target for the pitcher, as

Fig. 9-3

illustrated in Figure 9-3. Because the catcher's mitt is so large, players may have difficulty holding a steady target with one hand, so be sure to show them how to place the free hand behind the mitt for additional support.

As with all catches, receiving the pitch concludes with trapping the ball. The best way to trap the ball is to cushion the catch by letting the pitch softly punch back the mitt, by sliding the free hand around the mitt, and by grasping the ball. This can be tricky. Stress to your players that it is most important to use the free hand for support and then to trap the ball. Tell them never to place the free hand in front of the mitt before the ball is in the glove.

Protect the Body

Two protection reactions catchers need to overcome are (a) closing the eyes and (b) turning the head. These reactions are natural protection devices that can be overcome only by catching pitches in competitive situations during each practice. To protect the body, catchers must wear a face mask with a throat protector, a chest protector, and leg guards. (It is recommended that boys also wear a cup.) However, this equipment will only protect the catcher if the catcher's head is held steady, facing the pitch (see Figure 9-4). If the catcher turns to the side, the head, neck, back, and legs will be exposed and could be injured.

Fig. 9-4

Coaching Points
for Receiving the Pitch

1. Extend the glove arm with elbow slightly bent.
2. Place the throwing hand behind the mitt.
3. Watch the ball.
4. Keep the head and body facing the pitch.

Blocking Pitches

Low Pitches

Low pitches present a special problem, because to catch them, the mitt must be turned around so the fingers point down, as shown in Figure 9-5. But not all low pitches can be caught; some can only be blocked. Pitches thrown in the dirt are difficult to see and more difficult to catch. To block these pitches, show your players how to drop onto both knees, place the mitt between the legs, and use the entire body to block the ball (see Figure 9-6). Remember the principal rule of fielding: Keep the ball in front.

Fig. 9-5

Fig. 9-6

Pitches to the Side

Pitches thrown off to the side are also difficult to catch, and reaching out with the mitt is not the most effective way to stop the ball. Study Figure 9-7 and show your players how to move the feet, shift to the side quickly, and get the body in front of the ball. The Shift Drill (9.1) is a very versatile drill that catchers can use to practice blocking low pitches and pitches thrown to the side.

Fig. 9-7

Coaching Points for Blocking the Pitch

1. Watch the ball.
2. Drop onto the knees or shift the body.
3. Place the mitt down to block the ball.
4. Keep the ball in front.

Teaching Progression
for Catching Pitches

1. Teach the proper stance.
2. Demonstrate how to hold and use the mitt.
3. Practice catching and throwing easy pitches.
4. Gradually progress to catching faster pitches.
5. Teach how to block pitches.
6. Practice catching in game situations.

Catching Drills

9.1 Shift Drill

Age: 9 years and up

Purpose: To help catchers learn to shift on pitches in the dirt

Equipment: Full catcher's equipment and sometimes no equipment

Procedure: Begin the drill by having catchers block imaginary pitches that come at them in the dirt, directly at their feet, and to either side. Initially, catchers should do this without equipment. When they feel comfortable moving up, down, and to the side, have them practice moving after imaginary pitches wearing their equipment. Once your catchers are able to move well while wearing their equipment, gradually progress from throwing easy ground balls to throwing actual pitches to them.

Baseball
Planning Guide

Now that you know how to teach baseball skills, you are probably eager to begin practice sessions. But unless you know how to design and conduct practices, your enthusiasm could end in frustration. To conduct an effective practice requires careful planning. Take the time to study this Planning Guide section of *Coaching Baseball Effectively*, and you will find practices more beneficial and enjoyable for your players—and you.

In this Planning Guide you will find information on how to explain the game of baseball, how to develop long-term seasonal plans and daily practice plans, how to create an environment that will enhance the presentation and practice of baseball skills, and how to evaluate your players' skills and your coaching practices. Just as the Coaching Guide was a practical explanation of how to teach baseball skills, this Planning Guide is a practical explanation of how to conduct effective practices.

In chapter 12 you will find seasonal plans and daily practice plans for three age groups: 6 to 8 years, 9 to 12 years, and 13 to 15 years. These plans include all of the skills needed to play baseball. The skills are taught at a slower rate for younger, less skilled players and at a faster rate for older, more mature players.

Part III: Presenting the Game to Your Players

Baseball is such a popular American game that most young people generally understand some game procedures. For example, they probably know that pitchers try to pitch the ball, batters try to hit the ball, and fielders try to field the ball. Your players, however, may not understand some of the fundamental features of baseball that are necessary for playing the game. This part of the Planning Guide presents a short history of baseball and focuses on how you can explain the parts of the playing field, the role of the umpire, balls and strikes, and the other rules that govern baseball game play.

Chapter 10: The History of Baseball

Baseball has long been considered America's national pastime. Popular belief credits Abner Doubleday with inventing a truly American game while in Cooperstown, New York, in 1839. However, the facts do not support this belief, for it is doubtful that Doubleday was in Cooperstown in 1839; plus baseball is not mentioned in his letters and memoirs of that time. It is more probable that the British game called Rounders is the origin of modern baseball. Even so, Cooperstown has been considered the home of baseball; thus, the Baseball Hall of Fame was established there in 1939 as part of a centennial celebration.

Rounders, baseball's actual forerunner, is a British children's game played on a field with four stones or posts, placed 12 to 20 yards apart, which marked the corners of a square. The basic version had a player called a pecker, or feeder, throw a ball to a player called a striker, who tried to hit it. If the ball was hit, the striker could run around the posts. But, if the striker missed the ball three times or was hit with a thrown ball between the posts, the striker was out.

Evolution of Baseball

In America the game went through several transformations. In 1845 Alexander Cartwright organized the volunteer fire fighters with whom he played and then transformed into the Knickerbocker Baseball Club of New York, the first formal baseball team. Cartwright also formalized the game by developing a set of standard rules, most of which are still used today. Three canvas bases were placed 90 ft apart, and flat, circular disks represented home plate and the pitcher's plate. Defensive players could no longer put out base runners by hitting them with a thrown ball; base runners had to be tagged out or forced out. An inning was over after the defensive players put out three batters. Each team had nine players, and the defensive positions were nearly identical to defensive positions today.

A few differences between Cartwright's version of baseball and the modern major league version stand out. The primary difference is the pitcher's objective. In the early version of baseball, pitchers tried to pitch the ball so it could be hit, tossing underhand about 45 ft from home plate. Games continued until one side had 21 runs, or *aces*, and batters were out if the fielder caught the ball on the first bounce as well as on the fly.

After a formal set of rules was established, baseball spread rapidly. Many New Yorkers and other New Englanders, including Alexander Cartwright, spurred by the 1849 gold rush, traveled to California, spreading the game as they went. The game caught on in the South during the Civil War when Union soldiers taught the game to Confederate prisoners.

In 1858 a group of amateur baseball clubs formed the National Association of Baseball Players. This group changed the rules by making the game 7 innings rather than playing to 21 aces. This was altered to 9 innings soon after. This change probably indicated that defensive play had become significantly better and that the game took too long when played to 21 runs.

The first professional baseball league, organized in 1871, initiated several other changes. The bunt was invented as another way to get on base; the infield fly rule was adopted after fielders discovered they could drop fly balls intentionally to get 2 easy outs; more protective gloves were introduced for fielders; and the catcher's mask was invented. Furthermore, batters could no longer wait for a pitch, umpires could call a strike if they thought the batter should have swung at the pitch, and players had to catch balls on the fly rather than the first bounce to put a batter out.

The real beginning of major league baseball was the formation of the National League of Professional Baseball Clubs in 1876. The pitcher still threw underhand 45 ft from the plate, and the batter could request a high or low pitch. Nine balls were required for a walk, although there was no formal strike zone. An unfair ball was a pitch not to the batter's specifications. Four strikes were an out.

During the first 15 years of the National League, officials experimented with rules to find the right balance between the offensive and defensive aspects of the game. By 1884 pitchers could throw overhand or sidearm. Soon afterward, batters couldn't ask for a particular pitch, and in 1889, the National League instituted the 4-ball, 3-strike count for walks and outs.

Other rule changes were gradually introduced, such as moving the pitcher further back, but the game in 1890 was almost identical to the game today. The only major recent change has been the introduction of the designated hitter, a rule allowing a team to use a ninth hitter to replace a player in the batting order. This rule was adopted by the American League in 1973 and is also used by many minor leagues, as well as college and high school teams.

Organized Youth Baseball

In the 1920s many different groups began organizing sports for children, including baseball. Groups such as the American Legion, church organizations, YMCAs, police athletic leagues, and local service groups formed baseball leagues. In 1939 Little League Baseball was formed in Williamsport, Pennsylvania. By 1949 there were 300 leagues in 11 states. The Little League program grew rapidly after an article by Carl Stotz entitled "Small Boy's Dream Come True" was published in the *Saturday Evening Post* that year. This article proclaimed the values of the program for young boys and emphasized the rewards reaped by communities that had already established Little League teams. Little League is still the most widely known private national youth sport body. Other youth baseball organizations such as PONY (Protect Our Nation's Youth) baseball and Babe Ruth Baseball were formed to expand the idea of Little League to older youngsters and to incorporate into baseball other ideas that organizers thought beneficial for children.

Of the 20 million children between 6 and 16 who participate in organized sports today, over half play baseball or its direct derivative, softball. The vast majority of these baseball teams are still organized by a variety of local and national agencies, and the coaches are primarily volunteers. Financial constraints make volunteers a necessity in youth sports. Books such as this can make the sport experience more beneficial and enjoyable for both the thousands of coaches and the millions of youngsters involved in youth league baseball.

Chapter 11: The Game of Baseball

Introducing Baseball

One of your responsibilities is to teach players baseball rules and regulations, some of which were explained in the Baseball Coaching Guide. Because baseball is such a popular game, your players will be familiar with some rules and terms, but playing competitive games requires more than a general understanding of some rules; players must understand each rule affecting baseball game play. As an adult, your experience and understanding of baseball is much better than your players', so some of the following material may seem unnecessary. But remember, this chapter is not intended to teach you baseball; it is intended to help you explain the game to beginning players whose first formal introduction to baseball may be through you.

To find out how complicated baseball rules are, just look through a rule book: There are hundreds of rules and regulations covering a multitude of situations. Do not worry, however, about covering all the rules presented in a rule book; those specific situations are included to help umpires control the game, and some situations even confuse umpires. What your players need to know are the basic rules concerning the playing field, the equipment, the teams, and the game procedures. This chapter presents this information in two ways: (a) in simple explanations your players can easily understand, and (b) in a stimulating question/answer session that actively includes your players in the learning process.

The Playing Field

Explain to your players that baseball is played on a field that is shaped like and called a *diamond*. This diamond shape is formed by the line extending from home plate to first base and the line from home plate to third base (see Figure 11-1). These lines, called *foul lines*, extend beyond the bases to the outfield fence and form a *V* at home plate.

Fair and Foul Territory

Be sure your players know the difference between fair and foul by explaining that the area inside the foul lines is called *fair territory*, and the area outside the foul lines is called *foul territory*. Balls hit within fair territory are considered "live" and must be played. Balls hit in foul territory are also live but need *not* be played.

Beginning players could become confused when a ball is first hit into fair territory but then rolls into foul territory. Explain that a ball that rolls into foul territory is foul unless it passes first base or third base before it rolls into foul territory (see Figure 11-2).

Within the playing field are the bases, home plate, and pitching rubber. Your players should understand that a ball that touches the bases, home plate, or pitching rubber is considered live and in fair territory, even if it hits a base and then bounces into foul territory.

Fig. 11-1

Fig. 11-2

Offense and Defense

The terms *offense* and *defense* refer to the role of each team during a game. The offense is the team up to bat, and the runners and batters are the offensive players. The team out in the field is the defensive team, and the players who field the ball are the defensive players. When the defensive team is able to put out three offensive players, the offensive team and defensive team switch positions.

Although you understand the concept of an inning, your players may not. Explain that innings are like turns playing offense and defense. Each time one team has played both offense and defense, 1 inning has been played. Most youth league baseball games last 7 innings. This means each team has seven chances to bat and seven chances to play the field.

Offensive and Defensive Objectives

Baseball is played by two teams, each composed of nine players. The objective of the offensive team is to hit a ball and run counterclockwise around the bases and back to home plate. The objective of the defensive team is to stop the offensive team from scoring by making 3 outs. Explain that (a) *runs* are scored when offensive players are able to move around all the bases and back to home plate; (b) an *out* is made when an offensive player is not able to advance; and (c) the winning team is the team with the most runs at the end of the game.

Balls and Strikes

Beginning players are interested in playing and having fun, so they will want to know how games begin. Tell your players games begin when a ball is pitched by a defensive player called the *pitcher*. This player pitches from a *pitching rubber* to an offensive player called the *batter*, who stands in a *batting box* near home plate.

Batting boxes are on both sides of home plate, and batters can stand in either box. If the ball is pitched over the plate between the batter's knees and armpits, the ball is called a *strike*, and this area is called the *strike zone* (see Figure 11-3).

Fig. 11-3

Batters can get strikes in several ways: first, when a batter does not hit a ball pitched in the strike zone; second, when the batter hits the ball into foul territory. This is called a *foul ball* and counts as a strike. The only time a foul ball does not count as a strike is when there are already 2 strikes on a batter. And finally, a strike is called when a batter swings at the ball and misses. After 3 strikes, the batter is out, but after 4 balls, the batter is awarded first base.

Baserunning

Baserunning can be confusing to beginning players, but it need not be. The bases must be run in order from the batter's box to first, to second, and to third base, then back to home plate, as shown in Figure 11-4. Bases are safe areas, so when a runner is touching a base, he or she cannot be put out; but when a runner is not touching a base, he or she can be put out.

Fig. 11-4

Base runners can also be *forced* to run to another base. For example, when batters hit a ball, they must run to first base, and when they are on first base and a ball is hit, they must run to second base. Two runners cannot be on one base at the same time. It is important that your players understand force situations because the defense can put out runners forced to a base simply by tagging the base before the runner does.

As another part of baserunning, your players should understand the *base paths*. Explain that the base paths are the distances directly between the bases—if a straight line were drawn between the bases, this would be the *baseline*. Runners can be called out if they run outside of the baseline to avoid being tagged with the ball.

Fig. 11-5

Interference and Obstructions

Occasionally, base runners and fielders get in each other's way. Even though these situations are frustrating and are sometimes difficult to avoid, they will occur less often if players understand the rules about interference and obstructions.

Explain that defensive players cannot get in the way of the base runner unless they are fielding the ball or making an out. When a defensive player gets in the way of the base runner, it is called an *obstruction*, and the base runner is allowed to reach that base safely (see Figure 11-6).

Fig. 11-6

Interference is called when runners get in the way of a defensive player fielding the ball or making an out. The base runner who interferes with a defensive player will be called out; furthermore, if the umpire decides that the interference prevented the defense from putting out another base runner, then that base runner is also out.

Fig. 11-7

The Infield Fly Rule

A rule that is difficult for young players to understand is the *infield fly rule*, which prevents the defensive team from making 2 outs by dropping an easy fly ball. Here is how the infield fly rule works: When runners are on first base and second base, or when the bases are *loaded* (a runner on each base) with less than 2 outs, and an easy fly ball is hit to the infield, the umpire will call "infield fly, batter is out." When an infield fly is called, the batter is automatically out, and the other base runners are not forced to the next base. The infield fly rule prevents the defensive team from letting the fly ball drop to the ground, forcing out runners at two bases (getting a *double play*).

Umpires

Umpires are the ultimate authority on rules and enforcement of the rules. The umpires are often seen as bad guys by players, coaches, and spectators because they are usually only noticed when they make a close call. Umpires decide whether a pitch is a strike or a ball, whether a hit is fair or foul, and whether a runner is safe or out. Like all people, umpires will make mistakes from time to time. What is important is how you as a coach react when you think the umpire made a mistake. Remember, you need to be a role model for your players. The rules state that no one should question the judgment of the umpire. But, if you think a rule was not properly enforced or is interpreted differently from the way you understand the rule, you are allowed to question the umpire. When you do question the umpire, ask for *time out* and stay calm. Do not interrupt the game by screaming and arguing.

Treat Umpires With Respect

Most likely your umpires are parents, other coaches, or players who also want to help young players have the opportunity to play baseball. They, like you, are volunteers, not professionals. They are trying to make the game more pleasant for you and your players. Help them by responding calmly and reasonably.

Know the Rules

As a youth baseball coach, you should understand the rules to baseball game play. If you do not have a rule book, ask your league for the official rules for your organization, or refer to the rules located in Appendix A.

Presenting the Rules and Procedures

A useful method to explain or to review the rules and procedures of baseball play is to have a question/answer session while on a baseball field or while watching a baseball game. Either situation provides active participation for your players; furthermore, learning will be greatly enhanced by becoming involved with a demonstration rather than by simply sitting and listening. For example, if you asked where the players are positioned, you could move players to each position.

Be creative and appeal positively to each player. Laughing or poking fun at players may hurt their self-confidence and make them hesitant to participate in the activity. If players do not know the answer to a question, explain the answer, and, if possible, demonstrate it for them.

Suggested Questions

The following questions have been designed to help you explain baseball game play. They are divided into four major areas of baseball: (a) the field, (b) the equipment, (c) the teams, and (d) game play. Ask each question and discuss the answer thoroughly before moving on. To prevent your players from becoming confused, these questions have been arranged in a purposeful progression, each question leading to the next.

Remember, the questions have not been designed to test your knowledge of baseball, but to help you explain baseball to *beginning* baseball players. If you wish to use other questions or another method to explain the game, feel free to do so. As a coach, you need to decide which method will help you best explain the game to your players at their level of understanding.

The Field

1. *Q:* What is another name for the baseball field?
   A: A baseball *diamond* is another name for the baseball field.
2. *Q:* Why is the field called a diamond?
   A: The field has the shape of a diamond.
3. *Q:* How many bases are used in baseball?
   A: Three bases and one home plate are used in baseball.
4. *Q:* Where are the bases located?
   A: First base is located down the right side of the field; third base is located down the left side of the field; and second base is located in between first base and third base. The bases are placed equal distances away from each other.
5. *Q:* Where are the *foul lines*?
   A: There are two foul lines. One foul line extends from home plate to first base and out to right field; the other foul line

extends from home plate to third base and out to left field.

6. *Q:* What is the difference between *fair* territory and *foul* territory?

   A: Fair territory is the field *inside* the foul lines. Foul territory is the field *outside* the foul lines.

7. *Q:* Where is the *infield*?

   A: The infield is inside the foul lines—between home plate and the bases.

8. *Q:* Where is the *outfield*?

   A: The outfield is within the foul lines—between the infield and the outfield fence.

9. *Q:* What does *out of play* mean?

   A: Out of play means the ball is hit or thrown outside of the playing field. When a ball is out of play, base runners cannot advance or be put out.

10. *Q:* What are the *dugouts*?

    A: The dugouts are where the teams sit and are located along the first base and third base sides of the playing field.

11. *Q:* Are the dugouts in fair territory, foul territory, or out of play?

    A: The dugouts are out of play.

Equipment

1. *Q:* What are the three parts to the bat?

   A: The bat has a barrel, a knob, and a handle. (Explain these parts and their uses to your players.)

2. *Q:* Why are gloves used?

   A: Gloves are used to help catch the ball.

3. *Q:* What is the difference between a *glove* and a *mitt*?

   A: Gloves are not as large as mitts.

4. *Q:* Which players can wear a mitt?

   A: Catchers and first basemen are the only players who can wear mitts.

5. *Q:* What equipment does a catcher wear?

   A: The catcher wears a facemask, a throat protector, a chest protector, a mitt, and leg protectors.

6. *Q:* What type of shoes are players allowed to wear?

   A: Players are allowed to wear tennis shoes, running shoes, or rubber-studded cleats.

Players cannot wear shoes with metal cleats.

The Teams

1. *Q:* How many players can play for each team?

   A: Each team can play 9 players at a time for fast-pitch and 10 players for slow-pitch.

2. *Q:* What does *offense* mean?

   A: Offense means a team tries to hit the ball, to run the bases, and to score runs.

3. *Q:* Where are the offensive players positioned?

   A: The offensive players are either up to bat or on the bases.

4. *Q:* What does *defense* mean?

   A: Defense means a team tries to prevent the offensive team from hitting the ball, from running the bases, and from scoring runs. The defense tries to "put out" the offensive team.

5. *Q:* Where are the defensive players positioned?

   A: The defensive players are the catcher and pitcher; first, second, and third basemen; the right, center, and left fielders; and the shortstop. (Move your players to these positions.)

Game Play

General

1. *Q:* How is a baseball game started?

   A: Baseball games begin when a ball is pitched. The pitcher begins each play by pitching a ball to a batter.

2. *Q:* What happens when a batter hits the ball?

   A: The batter tries to run the bases.

3. *Q:* What is an *umpire*?

   A: Umpires are the officials who control the game, call balls and strikes, call players out and safe, and make sure the game is played properly. Umpires are on the field to help you have fun playing baseball.

4. *Q:* What does a *live ball* mean?

   A: Play is live when the umpire calls "Play ball," and the game is in progress.

5. *Q:* What does a *dead ball* mean?
   A: Play is dead when an umpire calls "Time out!" Play is also dead when a ball is hit foul or out of play. A dead ball means the game is not in progress, so runners cannot advance or be put out.
6. *Q:* What is an *out*?
   A: Players are out when they are unable to hit a ball or reach a base safely. When players are out, they must leave the field until their next turn at bat.
7. *Q:* What is a *tag-out*?
   A: A tag-out is touching the base runner with the ball when the runner is not on a base.
8. *Q:* What is a *force-out*?
   A: A force-out is touching a base while holding the ball before the runner reaches the base. Force-outs can be made only when a runner *must* run to a base.
9. *Q:* What is a *fly-out*?
   A: A fly-out is catching a ball on the fly or before it touches any part of the field. Batters are automatically "out" when a fly ball is caught.
10. *Q:* What is an *inning*?
    A: An inning is each team's opportunity to bat and to play the field. The offensive team gets to bat until 3 outs are made, then the defensive team gets to bat.
11. *Q:* How many innings are in each game?
    A: This answer will depend on your league rules. Each game usually has 7 innings. However, many youth leagues play 5-inning games.

Pitching and Batting

1. *Q:* Are balls pitched *underhand* or *overhand*?
   A: Balls are pitched overhand.
2. *Q:* Where do batters stand?
   A: Batters stand in the *batter's box*. A batter's box is located to the left- and right-hand side of home plate. (Move two players to the batter's box.)
3. *Q:* Can batters step out of the batter's box to hit a ball?

A: No! Batters are called out if they step outside of the batter's box to hit a ball.
4. *Q:* What is the *strike zone*?
   A: The strike zone begins at a batter's knees and extends to the batter's armpits.
5. *Q:* What is a *strike*?
   A: A strike is (a) a ball that has crossed home plate within the strike zone, (b) a swing and miss, and (c) a foul ball.
6. *Q:* How many strikes can a batter get before being called out?
   A: Batters are called out after they have made 3 strikes.
7. *Q:* What is a *ball*?
   A: A ball is a pitch that does not cross the strike zone.
8. *Q:* How many balls can a batter get before going to first base?
   A: Batters can go to first base after they have been pitched 4 balls.
9. *Q:* Can pitchers *fake* a pitch?
   A: No! Pitchers must pitch to the batter. A fake is ruled an illegal pitch and is called a balk.

Baserunning and Fielding

1. *Q:* Are the bases run in any particular order?
   A: Yes! The bases must be run in the following order: first base, second base, third base, and home plate. When runners want to return to a base, they must run the bases in reverse order: from third to second to first. Runners cannot cut across the field.
2. *Q:* What is a *baseline*?
   A: The baseline is the path directly between two bases. Base runners must run along this baseline.
3. *Q:* What happens if base runners run outside of the baseline to avoid being tagged out?
   A: Base runners are called out when they run outside of the baseline to avoid being tagged out.
4. *Q:* Which base can be *overrun*?
   A: Base runners can run past (overrun) first base without being tagged out.

5. *Q:* Why do runners have to touch a base?

   A: Bases are considered safe territory. Base runners cannot be called out while they are touching a base.

6. *Q:* Can base runners leave a base at any time?

   A: Yes! In most leagues base runners can play off a base. (Find out if your league has exceptions to this rule.)

7. *Q:* What must base runners do if they leave a base before a fly ball is caught?

   A: Base runners cannot leave a base until a fly ball is caught. If they leave the base early, they must return and touch that base before they can run to the next base. This is called *tagging up.*

8. *Q:* What is *interference?*

   A: Base runners cannot hinder a fielder from catching a ball or from making a play. When base runners hinder a fielder, it is called interference, and the base runner will be out.

9. *Q:* What is *obstruction?*

   A: Obstruction is blocking a base runner. When this happens, the base runner is able to move to the next base.

10. *Q:* Why are there *base coaches?*

    A: Base coaches are used to help base runners run the bases. One base coach is at first base and one base coach is at third base. Base coaches tell runners to stop at a base or to run to another base.

Game Play Drills

The Playing Rules Drill (11.1) can be used to teach your players the rules and game play of baseball. We suggest you modify this drill to meet the needs of your team and to correspond with the rules of your baseball league. Conduct the Playing Rules Drill as indicated below:

(11.1) Playing Rules Drill

Age: 9 years and up

Purpose: To teach players the rules of baseball using practical and meaningful situations. This drill can be used to explain all playing rules.

Equipment: Balls, bats, one set of bases

Procedure: Select the rules you wish to teach prior to beginning this drill. Once the rules have been selected, simply and clearly explain the rules to the players. Then set up practical situations to illustrate the rules. For example: "When a ball is touched in foul territory before it reaches first or third base, the ball is foul. This means the batter and any base runners cannot run the bases." To illustrate this rule, have your players line up near one of the foul lines while you roll balls fair and foul. Let your players call out the fair and the foul balls.

Part IV: Planning Your Practice Sessions

Practice sessions are the most important part of the baseball season. These are the times once or twice a week your players receive detailed instruction, practice their skills, develop new friendships with their teammates, and, hopefully, have fun playing baseball. Your preparation for each practice is vital to the success of every practice session. Conducting effective practices does not just happen but requires an *understanding* of baseball skills, of how to teach beginning baseball players, and of how to develop practice plans. Just as a highly skilled athlete who has practiced hard for many years makes difficult plays appear easy, careful planning will ensure that each practice is fun, effective, and easy to conduct.

If you are like most volunteer coaches, you probably have a full-time job, a home to care for, children to raise, and bills to pay. When you do have time to think about coaching a baseball team, you probably do not have the 2 or 3 hours required to develop next week's practice plans,

let alone a plan for teaching skills throughout the season. We understand these time commitments, but we still want you to have carefully planned practice sessions. That is why we have included a set of seasonal plans and practice plans for you, fully developed and ready to use. These plans incorporate the coaching points, teaching progressions, and drills presented in the Baseball Coaching Guide and can be modified to meet the specific needs of your team.

Also included in part II are suggestions for modifying the game of baseball for younger players and for what is necessary to prepare for each game.

Even with the best planning, not every practice will be trouble-free. You will need to resolve disputes, punish and reward players, and adjust practices according to the weather and field conditions. All of this valuable information contained in the ACEP Level 1 coaching book, *Coaching Young Athletes*, will help you be a more effective coach.

Chapter 12: Instructional Schedules and Practice Plans

Grouping Players

It is important you recognize that young people of the same age will not be of equal skill or physical maturation. Some 10-year-olds may be small, uncoordinated, and unable to participate effectively in a structured environment such as a controlled practice. Other 10-year-olds will be much larger, better skilled, and eager to be instructed as to what they should do in practice.

Consequently, it is not always fair to place young people who are the same age in the same leagues. Youngsters will benefit more by working with other children similar in size and skill than with players who are similar in age. We recommend highly, if it is at all possible, that you group young people according to size and skill, not age.

Suggested Game Modifications

As you read in chapter 10, "The History of Baseball," this is a game created by and for adults. The distances between bases and between pitching rubber and home plate were created for adults. Also, the skills of hitting and pitching, which are not always easy for many adults, are especially difficult for young players. Just as players should be grouped according to their size and skill, the game should be modified based upon the size and skill of the players.

We consulted with several youth leagues and national organizations to determine if certain modifications could help young, beginning players have more fun playing baseball. After this, we considered the maturational development and skill levels of children between 6 years (less mature) and 15 years (more mature). The following game modifications were then developed to help young, beginning players develop baseball skills while they have fun playing baseball. We encourage you to study these rule modifications and use them in your league.

Age	Modifications
5-7	Bases: 50 ft apart.
	Pitching position: 40 ft from home plate; pitcher only has fielding responsibilities.
	Batting: Use a batting tee. Everyone bats once each inning in a 4-inning game.
	Baserunning: No stealing.
8-9	Bases: 60 ft apart.
	Pitching position: 44 ft from home plate; offensive coaches pitch to their batters.

Batting: No walks allowed; no bunting.

Baserunning: No stealing.

10-12   Bases: 70 ft apart.

Pitching position: 48 ft from home plate; opposing pitcher pitches.

13-15   Bases: 80 ft apart.

Pitching position: 54 ft from home plate.

Instructional Schedules for Teaching and Refining Skills

You will need to develop a seasonal plan to teach baseball skills effectively and to follow the teaching progressions presented in the Baseball Coaching Guide. A seasonal plan is an overview of what will be accomplished during the season. Developing seasonal plans will help you determine your team's status at the beginning of a season and the progress of your team at various points throughout the season.

4-Week Instructional Schedule for Youth Baseball Ages 6-8

Goal: To help players learn and practice the individual and team skills needed to play a regulation game after 4 weeks.

T(10): Teach and practice the skill initially in 10 min.　　　　*: These skills are practiced during the drills
P(10): Review and practice the skill for 10 min.

Skills	Week 1 Day 1	Day 2	Week 2 Day 3	Day 4	Week 3 Day 5	Day 6	Week 4 Day 7	Day 8	Time in Minutes
Warm-up Exercises	T(5)	P(5)	P(5)	P(5)	P(5)	P(5)	P(5)	P(5)	40
Cool-down Exercises	T(5)	P(5)	P(5)	P(5)	P(5)	P(5)	P(5)	P(5)	40
Throwing/Catching									
Throwing motion	T(10)	*	*		*	*		*	10
Catching throws	T(10)	*	*		*	*		*	10
Skip and throw				T(10)	*	*		*	10
Drills		P(10)	P(10)		P(10)	P(5)		P(5)	40
Fielding									
Ground balls	T(10)	*	*			*	*	*	10
Fly balls			T(10)				*	*	10
Basket catch					T(10)		*	*	10
Drills		P(10)	P(10)				P(10)	P(10)	40
Batting									
Swinging a bat	T(10)	*				*			10
Hitting off a tee		T(10)			*		*		10
Drills		P(5)			P(10)	P(5)	P(10)		30
Baserunning									
First base		T(10)					*		10
Rounding bases			T(10)	*		*	*		10
Drills				P(10)		P(10)	P(10)		30
Positional Skills									
Coverage areas		T(10)		*			*	*	10
Backing up					T(10)		*	*	10
Drills				P(10)			P(10)	P(5)	25
Relaying the Ball					T(10)		P(10)		20
Game Play									
Baseball rules			T(10)						10
Game play				T(10)					10
Practice games				P(10)		P(30)			40

A good seasonal plan teaches fundamental skills and progresses to more advanced skills. For instance, you would want to teach the batting grip before you teach how to swing the bat.

Similarly, you would not want to teach your players positional coverage and responsibilities before you teach them how to wear and use their gloves properly.

4-Week Instructional Schedule for Youth Baseball Ages 9-12

Goal: To help players learn and practice the individual and team skills needed to play a regulation game after 4 weeks.

T(10): Teach and practice the skill initially for 10 min.
P(10): Review and practice the skill for 10 min.

*: These skills are practiced during the drills.

| Skills | Week 1 | | Week 2 | | Week 3 | | Week 4 | | Time in |
	Day 1	Day 2	Day 3	Day 4	Day 5	Day 6	Day 7	Day 8	Minutes
Throwing/Catching									
Throwing motion	T(10)	*							10
Catching throws	T(10)	*							10
Skip and throw			T(10)		*				10
Drills		P(10)			P(15)				25
Fielding									
Ground balls	T(10)	*	*		*	*	*	*	10
Fly balls		T(10)	*		*	*	*	*	10
Basket catch					T(15)	*	*	*	15
Drills			P(10)		P(20)	P(20)	P(15)	P(10)	75
Batting									
Swinging	T(10)	*		*	*		*		10
Bunting			T(10)	*			*		10
Drills		P(10)		P(10)	P(20)		P(15)		55
Baserunning									
First base		T(10)				*			10
Rounding bases			T(10)			*			10
Leaving/Tag-ups				T(10)		*			10
Sliding							T(15)	*	15
Drills						P(20)		P(10)	30
Positional Skills									
Coverage areas	T(10)		*				*		10
Force/Tag-outs				T(10)			*		10
Backing up		T(10)	*				*		10
Drills'			P(10)				P(15)	P(10)	35
Team Defense									
Relays/Cut-offs			T(10)				*		10
Bunt coverage					T(10)		*		10
Drills							P(15)		15
Game Play									
Baseball rules	T(10)								10
Playing a game		T(10)							10
Playing strategy				T(10)					10
Practice games						P(40)		P(30)	70
Pitching			T(10)	P(10)	P(20)	P(20)		P(10)	70
Catching									
Catching pitches			T(10)	P(10)	P(10)	P(10)		*	40
Blocking pitches						T(10)	*	*	10
Drills					P(10)		P(10)	P(10)	30

4-Week Instructional Schedule for Youth Baseball Ages 13 and Up

Goal: To help players learn and practice the individual and team skills needed to play a regulation game after 4 weeks.

T(10): Teach skill for first time in 10 min.
P(10); Practice or drill the skill for 10 min.

*: These skill components are practiced during the drills for this playing category.

Skills	Week 1		Week 2		Week 3		Week 4		Time in Minutes
	Day 1	Day 2	Day 3	Day 4	Day 5	Day 6	Day 7	Day 8	
Throwing/Catching									
Throwing motion	T(10)	*	*						10
Catching throws	T(10)	*	*						10
Skip and throw			T(10)						10
Drills		P(10)		P(10)					20
Fielding									
Ground balls	T(15)					*	*	*	15
Fly balls		T(15)				*	*	*	15
Basket catch			T(15)			*	*	*	15
Drills					P(15)	P(5)	P(15)	P(20)	55
Batting									
Swinging a bat	T(15)	*				*	*		15
Bunting			T(15)			*	*		15
Placing hits					T(15)	*	*		15
Drills		P(10)				P(15)	P(30)		55
Baserunning									
First base		T(10)				*			10
Rounding bases		T(10)				*			10
Leaving/Tag-ups				T(15)		*			15
Sliding					T(15)				15
Drills						P(10)			10
Positional Skills									
Coverage areas	T(10)		*		*				10
Force/Tag-outs				T(15)	*			*	15
Backing up		T(10)	*		*			*	10
Drills			P(15)		P(15)			P(10)	40
Team Defense									
Relays/Cut-offs			T(20)				*	*	20
Bunt coverage				T(10)			*	*	10
Double plays					T(20)		*	*	20
Drills							P(20)	P(10)	30
Game Play									
Baseball rules	T(10)								10
Playing a game		T(15)							15
Playing strategy				T(15)					15
Practice games						P(40)		P(40)	80
Pitching			T(15)	P(15)	P(15)	P(15)	P(20)	P(20)	100
Catching									
Catching pitches			T(15)	*	*	*	*	*	15
Blocking pitches						T(10)	*	*	10
Drills				P(15)	P(15)	P(10)	P(15)	P(20)	75

Three examples of how to use your seasonal plan outline to develop a series of practices are presented below. These plans cover the age ranges of (a) 6 to 8 years (less mature), (b) 9 to 12 years (moderately mature), and (c) 13 to 15 years (more mature). They also span a 4-week period with two practices each week, for a total of eight practice sessions. Because these plans do not cover an entire season, we have called them *instructional schedules*, rather than seasonal plans.

These instructional schedules can be used in their present form, but they are intended to serve as general guides rather than as strict plans. If you find your players require more or less time to learn and to refine these skills, then you should adjust the presentation and practice times to meet the needs of your players. After the first 4 weeks of your season, use the format of the instructional schedules to develop additional long-term plans. By taking the time to study and use these instructional schedules, developing additional schedules will take far less time and will be easy to use.

Daily Practice Plans

The following daily practice plans correspond with the instructional schedules: There are eight practice sessions covering 4 weeks of the season. One set of plans is written for less mature players (about 6 to 8 years), the second set is for moderately mature players (about 9 to 12 years), and the third set is for more mature players (about 13 to 15 years). While these plans can be used without any changes, they will not be perfect for every team. When you modify these practice plans, be receptive to the input of your assistant coaches and your players. Assistant coaches may be able to observe some things you cannot and your players will soon know which skills they need to practice and the drills that they enjoy.

The Practice Plan Format

Each practice plan has been designed to be taken onto the practice field and specifies the following:

- The amount of time needed for each practice
- The activities focused on during each practice
- The organization needed to conduct drills
- Coaching points to better teach your players

First, an overview of the entire practice is presented: The number of the practice, total practice time, instructional goals, drills, and equipment are included in this overview. The actual practice plan follows with time divisions, activities, organization, and coaching points specified.

The Component/Time column specifies (a) whether the skill is to be taught or practiced, (b) the length in minutes for the activity, and (c) the elapsed practice time through that activity. The Activity/Drills column indicates the skill activities to be taught or practiced and the recommended drills for practicing those skills. Points for keeping everyone active and organized are included in the Organization column. Finally, hints to help you better teach and correct skills are found in the column labeled Coaching Points.

To obtain the best results from every practice, each plan includes the following components from the ACEP Level 1 book, *Coaching Young Athletes*:

- Warming up
- Practicing previously taught skills
- Teaching and practicing new skills
- Practicing in game-like situations
- Cooling down
- Evaluating practice

These components need not be in this order, but they should be a part of each practice session. For example, teaching and practicing new skills are more important for the first few sessions than reviewing previously taught skills. Later in the season reviewing previously taught skills and practicing in gamelike situations is more important than teaching new skills. But your players will need to warm up, cool down, and practice in gamelike situations each practice.

Using the Drills

Every drill included in the practice plans can be found in the Drills section of each chapter in this book. The number at the end of each drill indicates the chapter in which the drill can be found and the number it is listed in that chapter. For example, The Practice Game Drill is Number 7.14. This means it is located in chapter 7 and is the 14th drill listed in that chapter.

Practice Plan 1

Age: 6-8
Total time: 70 minutes

Instructional Goals
Teach warm-up and cool-down exercises. Teach fundamentals of throwing, catching, fielding ground balls, and batting from a tee.

Equipment
Balls, bats, batting tees
For the coach: Player roster, practice plans, first-aid kit

Drills
Throwing—Ball Grip Drill; Flick the Ball Drill
Catching—Players pair up, throw and catch
Fielding—Fielding Position Drill; Fielding Ground Balls Drill
Batting—Swinging the Bat Drill

Component/Time	Activity/Drills	Organization	Coaching Points
Introduction 5 min	Meet players; check the roster.	Bring the team together.	Introduce the coaches. State your goals and expectations.
Teach 5 min (10 min)	Stretch, jog, and throw	Organize the team in a circle. Demonstrate from inside the circle.	Stretch slowly; do not bounce. Jog; do not run hard. Throw from a moderate distance.
Teach 20 min (30 min)	Throwing and Catching Ball Grip Drill Flick the Ball Drill Throw and catch	Bring the team together. Pair up players for drills. Pairs stand apart a moderate distance.	Demonstrate the grip, step, armswing, and follow-through. Look at the target and follow through.
Teach 15 min (45 min)	Batting Swing the Bat Drill	Bring the team together. Pair up players for drills. Spread apart and alternate players swinging with and without bats.	Demonstrate the grip, stance, stride, and armswing. Stress watching the ball and following through.
Teach 15 min (60 min)	Fielding Ground Balls Fielding Position Fielding Ground Balls Drill	Bring the team together. Pair up players for drills. Pairs stand apart a moderate distance.	Demonstrate the stance and glove position. Stress watching the ball and trapping the ball.
Teach/Cool-down 5 min (65 min)	Easy jogging, throwing, and stretching	Pair up for throws. Jog as a group. Stretch in a group circle.	Do not run hard. Throw easy. Stretch slowly; do not bounce.
Review/ Evaluation 5 min (70 min)	Review the skills taught today. Comment on practice performance.	Bring the team together. Watch your time; do not drag on.	Be positive and constructive. Compliment effort. Mention the time and place for next practice.

Practice Plan 2

Age: 6-8
Total time: 70 minutes

Instructional Goals
Review and practice the warm-up and cool-down exercises, throwing, fielding ground balls, and batting skills. Teach running to first base, and positional areas and responsibilities.

Equipment
Balls, bats, batting tees, complete set of bases, 2 first bases, batting helmets
For the coach: Player roster, practice plans, first-aid kit

Drills
Throwing/Catching—Flick the Ball Drill; Throw and catch
Fielding—Fielding Position Drill; Fielding Ground Balls Drill
Batting—Hitting Off a Tee Drill; Swinging the Bat Drill
Baserunning—Running to First Base Drill

Component/Time	Activity/Drills	Organization	Coaching Points
Introduction 5 min	Greet your players; check your roster. Tell players about today's practice.	Bring the team together.	Be prompt and enthusiastic. Briefly describe the practice.
Warm-up 5 min (10 min)	Easy stretching, jogging, and throwing	Organize the team in a circle. Lead stretching in the circle. Jog as a group. Pair up for throws.	Stretch slowly; do not bounce. Jog; do not run hard. Throw from a moderate distance.
Review/Practice 10 min (20 min)	Throwing/Catching Flick the Ball Drill Throw and catch	Review in large group. Pair up players for drills. Pairs stand apart a moderate distance.	Emphasize the proper grip, stride, and arm swing. Correct skills as players practice.
Review/Practice 10 min (30 min)	Fielding Ground Balls Fielding Position Drill Fielding Ground Balls Drill	Review in large group. Pair up players for drills. Pairs stand apart a moderate distance.	Emphasize the proper body and glove position. Stress watching and trapping the ball.
Review/Practice 10 min (40 min)	Batting Hitting Off a Tee Drill Swinging a Bat Drill	Review in a large group. Divide team in half for drills. One group practices swings while the other hits off tees.	Emphasize the proper grip, stance, bat swing, and follow-through. Watch the ball and swing level.
Teach 10 min (50 min)	Baserunning Running Past First Base Drill	Teach in a large group. Set up 2 first bases. Divide team in half for the drill.	Have players run half the distance only. Stress running past the base and touching the front edge of the base.
Teach 10 min (60 min)	Positional coverage areas and responsibilities Throw balls to players at each position	Teach in a large group. Divide in half for practice. Rotate the players around each position.	Stress the coverage areas. Be sure each player fields at each position.
Cool-down 5 min (65 min)	Easy throwing, jogging, and stretching	Bring the team together. Pair up for throws. Jog as a group. Stretch in a circle.	Throw easy. Do not run fast. Stretch slowly; do not bounce.
Evaluation 5 min (70 min)	Review the practice	Discuss as a group.	Be positive and constructive. Compliment hustle and effort. Review areas that need work.

Practice Plan 3

Age: 6-8
Total time: 60 minutes

Instructional Goals
Review and practice throwing/catching and fielding ground balls. Teach fielding fly balls, running around the bases, and baseball rules.

Equipment
Balls, 1 set of bases (2 first bases), rule book
For the coach: Player roster, practice plans, first-aid kit

Drills
Throwing/Catching—Ball Grip Drill; Throwing for Points Drill
Fielding—Fielding Ground Balls Drill; Judging Fly Balls Drill
Baserunning—Rounding First Base Drill
Baseball Rules—Playing Rules Drill

Component/Time	Activity/Drills	Organization	Coaching Points
Introduction 5 min	Easy stretching, jogging, throwing	Stretch in a team circle. Jog as a group. Pair up for throws.	Check roster and discuss today's practice.
Practice 10 min (15 min)	Throwing/Catching Ball Grip Drill Throw and Catch	Pair up players. Players stand apart a moderate distance.	Emphasize striding toward the target, snapping the wrist, and the follow-through.
Teach/Practice 15 min (30 min)	Fielding Ground Balls Fielding Ground Balls Drill Judging Fly Balls Drill	Bring players together and teach in large group. Pair up players for drills.	Move to the ball. Watch the ball. Trap with free hand.
Teach 15 min (45 min)	Baserunning Rounding First Base Drill	Teach in a large group. Set up 2 first bases. Divide the team in half for the drill.	Swing to the outside, turn into the base, touch the inside corner of the base.
Teach 10 min (55 min)	Playing Rules Playing Rules Drill	Teach in a large group. Include players in the activity.	Be thorough, but do not drag on. Be positive and encourage player's participation.
Cool-down/ Evaluation 5 min (60 min)	Easy throwing, jogging, stretching	Pair up for throwing. Jog as a group. Stretch in a group circle.	Cool down easily. Evaluate the practice. Mention time and place for next practice.

Practice Plan 4

Age: 6-8
Total time: 60 minutes

Instructional Goals
Review the skill of running around the bases and the positional coverage areas. Teach the skip and throw and how to play a game.

Equipment
Balls, bats, batting tees, helmets, 2 sets of bases, rule book
For the coach: Player roster, practice plans, first-aid kit

Drills
Baserunning—Running the Bases Drill
Positional Areas—Individual Position Drill
How to Play Baseball—Playing Rules Drill; practice game drill
Skip and Throw—Step and Throw Drill

Component/Time	Activity/Drills	Organization	Coaching Points
Introduction/ Warm-up 5 min	Easy stretching, jogging, throwing	Stretching in a team circle. Jog as a group. Pair up for throws.	Check roster and discuss today's practice.
Practice 10 min (15 min)	Baserunning Running the Bases Drill	Set up 2 diamonds. Divide the team in half.	Swing wide, turn into the base, touch the inside corner of the base.
Teach 10 min (25 min)	The Skip and Throw Step and Throw Drill	Teach the skill in a large group. Pair up players for the drill. Players stand apart a moderate distance.	Demonstrate the skip, the step, then the throw. Step at the target and follow through.
Practice 10 min (35 min)	Positional Areas Individual Position Drill	Divide the team in half. Have the groups practice on separate diamonds.	Stress making plays at each position. Back up other positions.
Teach 20 min (55 min)	How to Play Baseball Playing Rules Drill Practice Game Drill	Conduct the Playing Rules Drill as a group. Divide the team in half for a 1-inning game.	Relate the rules to actual game play. Keep the game fun.
Cool-down/ Evaluation 5 min (60 min)	Easy throwing, jogging, stretching	Throw in pairs. Jog as a large group. Stretch in a group circle.	Evaluate the practice. Let them know you had fun today. Mention time and place for next practice.

Practice Plan 5

Age: 6-8
Total time: 60 minutes

Instructional Goals
Review the skip and throw. Practice batting off a tee. Teach the basket catch, backing up other players, and relaying the ball.

Equipment
Balls, bats, batting tees, 2 sets of bases
For the coach: Player roster, practice plans, first-aid kit

Drills
The Skip and Throw—Throwing for Points Drill
Batting—Hitting Off a Tee Drill
Fielding—Basket Catch Drill
Positional Skills—Reduced Field Playing Drill
Team Defense—Cut-off and Relay Drill

Component/Time	Activity/Drills	Organization	Coaching Points
Introduction/ Warm-up 5 min	Easy stretching, jogging, throwing	Lead stretches in a group circle. Jog as a group. Pair up to throw.	Check roster and discuss today's practice.
Review/Practice 10 min (15 min)	The Skip and Throw Thowing for Points Drill	Review in large group. Pair up players for Rhythm Drill.	Emphasize hopping onto and pushing off the back foot.
Practice 10 min (25 min)	Batting Hitting Off a Tee Drill	Pair up players. While one player bats, the other player watches for proper form.	Look for the batter striding straight ahead, swinging level, and following through.
Teach (10 min (35 min)	Fielding Fly Balls Basket Catch Drill	Teach in a large group. Divide team in half for practice.	Throw short fly balls. Palm of glove faces upward. Watch the ball; trap the ball.
Teach 10 min (45 min)	Backing Up Players Reduced Playing Field Drill	Teach in a large group. Divide team into groups for drill. Have players move to back up other fielders.	Position players 10 ft behind the fielder. Stand in the ready position.
Teach 10 min (55 min)	Relays Cut-off and Relay Drill	Teach in a large group. Divide into groups of 3-5 players for the drill.	Use the skip and throw. Throw accurately, not fast.
Cool-down/ Evaluation 5 min (60 min)	Easy throwing, jogging, stretching	Bring everyone together. Pair up for throwing. Jog as a group. Stretch in a group circle.	Provide feedback during cool-down. Praise effort and attention. A game is planned for next practice.

Practice Plan 6

Age: 6-8
Total time: 60 minutes

Instructional Goals
Practice all skills taught previously. Play a practice game. Prepare for game by throwing, catching, fielding, batting, and baserunning.

Equipment
Balls, bats, batting tees, 1 set of bases
For the coach: Player roster, practice plans, first-aid kit

Drills
Preparation for the Game—Throwing and catching; Ground Ball-Fly Ball Drill; Swinging the Bat Drill; Running the Bases Drill

Component/Time	Activity/Drills	Organization	Coaching Points
Introduction/ Warm-up 5 min	Easy stretching, jogging, throwing	Stretch in a group circle. Jog as a group. Pair up for throwing.	Check roster and discuss today's practice.
Practice 20 min (25 min)	Game Preparation　Throwing and catching　Ground Ball-Fly Ball Drill　Swinging the Bat Drill　Running the Bases Drill	Divide drills among coaches (2 drills for 2 coaches). Divide team in 4 groups. Rotate players through each drill.	Watch for proper form. Keep the players organized. Watch your time.
Practice 30 min (55 min)	Practice Game　Practice Game Drill	Divide team in half. Players choose and play 2 positions.	Control the game. Give feedback, but let them play and have fun.
Cool-down/ Evaluation 5 min (60 min)	Easy throwing, jogging, stretching	Cool-down as a group.	Evaluate practice. Mention time and place for next practice. Be constructive and enthusiastic.

Practice Plan 7

Age: 6-8
Total time: 60 minutes

Instructional Goals
Review and practice the skills of fielding, batting, baserunning, positional play, and relaying the ball.

Equipment
Balls, bats, batting tees, 1 set of bases
For the coach: Player roster, practice plans, first-aid kit

Drills
Fielding—Ground Ball-Fly Ball Drill
Batting—Hitting Off a Tee Drill
Baserunning—Running the Bases Drill
Positional Play—Reduced Field Playing Drill
Relaying the Ball—Cut-off and Relay Drill

Component/Time	Activity/Drills	Organization	Coaching Points
Introduction Warm-up 5 min	Easy stretching, jogging, throwing	Stretch in a group circle. Jog as a group. Pair up for throwing.	Check the roster; review today's practice.
Practice 10 min (15 min)	Fielding Ground Ball-Fly Ball Drill	Divide the team in half. Have one group field while the other bats. Switch after 5 min.	Watch the ball; move to the ball; trap the ball in the glove.
Practice 10 min (25 min)	Batting Hitting Off a Tee Drill	Divide the team in half. Have one group bat while the other fields.	Use the proper stance. Stride into the hit; watch the ball; swing level; follow through.
Practice 20 min (45 min)	Baserunning Running the Bases Drill	Divide the team in half. One group runs while the other plays positions. Switch after 10 min.	First base—Touch the front edge; run past the base; do not leap upon the base. Around the bases—Swing wide; turn into the base; touch the inside corner.
	Positional Play Reduced Playing Field Drill	Divide the team in half. Have one group practice positions while the other runs bases. Have players practice 2 positions.	Use proper fielding mechanics. Move on each play and back up other players.
Practice 10 min (55 min)	Relaying the Ball Cut-off and Relay Drill	Form groups of 3-5 players. Players stand apart a moderate distance.	Throw accurately, not fast. Use the skip and throw.
Cool-down/ Evaluation 5 min (60 min)	Easy throwing, jogging, stretching	Pair up for throws. Jog as a group. Stretch in a group circle.	Evaluate the practice. Be positive and constructive. Mention time and place for next practice.

Practice Plan 8

Instructional Goals
Practice all skills taught previously by playing a practice game. Prepare for the game by throwing, fielding, and practicing positional play.

Equipment
Balls, bats, batting tees, 1 set of bases
For the coach: Player roster, practice plans, first-aid kit

Drills
Preparation for the Game—Ground Ball-Fly Ball Drill; Throwing for Points Drill; Individual Position Drill

Component/Time	Activity/Drills	Organization	Coaching Points
Introduction/ Warm-up 5 min	Easy stretching, jogging, throwing	Stretch in a group circle. Jog as a group. Pair up for throws.	Check the roster and discuss today's practice.
Practice 20 min (25 min)	Game Preparation Drills Ground Ball-Fly Ball Drill Individual Position Drill Throwing for Points Drill	Divide the team in 3 groups: One group fields, one practices positional play, one throws for points. Rotate players through the drills.	Fielding—Watch the ball; move to the ball; trap the ball. Positional Play—Play 2 positions; back up other players; throw accurately.
Practice 30 min (55 min)	Practice Game Practice Game Drill	Divide team in half. Set up the diamond.	Have fun. Compliment effort and hustle. Correct skills constructively.
Cool-down/ Evaluation 5 min (60 min)	Easy throwing, jogging, stretching	Pair up for throws. Jog as a group. Stretch in a group circle.	Let them know you had fun. Mention time and place of first game. Review skills to work on before the game.

Practice Plan 1

Instructional Goals
Teach the fundamental skills of throwing, catching, fielding, and batting. Introduce players to playing positions and baseball rules.

Equipment
Balls, bats, 1 set of bases, helmets
For the coach: Player roster, practice plans, first-aid kit

Drills
Throwing—Ball Grip Drill; Throwing Action Drill
Catching—Throwing and catching
Fielding—Fielding Position Drill; Fielding Ground Balls Drill
Batting—Simulating Swings Drill; Hitting Off a Tee Drill
Baseball Rules—Playing Rules Drill

Component/Time	Activity/Drills	Organization	Coaching Points
Introduction 5 min	Introduce yourself and other coaches. Check the roster. Talk about how you will coach the team.	Bring the players together.	Be enthusiastic. Let them know you care about learning skills and about having fun.
Warm-up 5 min (10 min)	Easy stretching, jogging, throwing	Stretch in a group circle. Jog as a group. Pair up for throws and stand apart a moderate distance.	Lead and demonstrate stretches from inside the circle. Stretch slowly; do not bounce. Jog easily; do not race. Do not throw fast.
Teach/Practice 10 min (20 min)	Throwing Motion Ball Grip Drill Throwing Action Drill	Teach in a group. Pair up players for drills.	Emphasize the grip, arm swing, stride, and follow-through. Throw accurately.
Teach/Practice 10 min (30 min)	Catch Throws Throw and catch	Teach in a group. Pair up for drill.	Present how to wear and use the glove. Watch the ball; trap the ball.
Teach/Practice 10 min (40 min)	Fielding Fielding Position Drill Fielding Ground Balls	Teach in a group. Practice fielding position individually. Pair up for fielding ground balls.	Emphasize proper leg and hand position. Move to the ball; watch the ball; trap the ball.
Teach/Practice 10 min (50 min)	Batting Simulating Swings Drill Hitting Off a Tee Drill	Teach in a group. Pair up for drills. Players alternate swinging and watching for correct form. Spread apart and hit off a tee into fence or net.	Present proper grip, stance, stride, arm swing, and follow-through. Watch the ball.
Teach/Practice 10 min (60 min)	Positional Coverage Areas Move players through positions	Teach in a group. Rotate players through each position on the field.	Stress knowing the playing areas and the responsibilities of each position.
Teach 10 min (70 min)	Baseball Game Rules Playing Rules Drill	Conduct question-and-answer session as a group. Involve your players in the presentation.	Explain the rules simply and clearly. Let your players show you their answers.
Teach/Cool-down 5 min (75 min)	Easy throwing, jogging, stretching	Pair up for throws. Jog as a group. Stretch in a group circle. Lead stretches from inside the circle.	Throw easy, not fast. Jog easily; do not race. Stretch slowly; do not bounce.
Evaluation 5 min (80 min)	Review today's practice	Bring the players together.	Be positive and constructive; review the skills. Mention time and place for next practice.

Practice Plan 2

Age: 9-12
Total time: 80 minutes

Instructional Goals
Review and practice throwing, catching and batting. Teach fielding fly balls, running to first base, back-up positions, and how to play a game.

Equipment
Balls, bats, batting tees, 2 sets of bases
For the coach: Player roster, practice plans, first-aid kit

Drills
Throwing/Catching—Throw and Catch; Throw and Step Back Drill
Batting—Hitting Off a Tee Drill or Simulating Swings Drill; Hitting Easy Pitches Drill
Fielding—Judging Fly Balls Drill
Baserunning—Running Past First Base Drill; Leaving the Batter's Box Drill
Backing-up—Backing-up Drill

Component/Time	Activity/Drills	Organization	Coaching Points
Introduction 5 min	Review the coaches' and players' names. Check the roster. Review your coaching philosophy.	Bring the players together.	Be enthusiastic. Let them know you care about learning skills and about having fun.
Review/Warm-up 5 min (10 min)	Easy stretching, jogging, throwing	Stretch in a group circle. Jog as a group. Pair up for throws and stand apart a moderate distance.	Lead and demonstrate stretches from inside the circle. Stretch slowly; do not bounce. Jog easily; do not race. Throw easy, not fast.
Review/Practice 10 min (20 min)	Throwing/Catching Throw and Catch Throw and Step Back Drill	Review throwing and catching fundamentals as a group. Pair up for drills.	Throwing—Proper grip, stride, follow-through. Catching—Glove control; watch and trap the ball.
Review/Practice 10 min (30 min)	Batting Hitting Off a Tee Drill, or Simulating Swings Drill Hit Easy Pitches Drill	Review as a group. Pair up for drills. If tees are not available, divide team in half. Practice swings and let players hit easy pitches.	Proper grip; swing level; watch the ball; stride forward and follow through.
Teach 10 min (40 min)	Fielding Fly Balls Judging Fly Balls Drill	Teach as a group. Divide team in half for drill.	Watch the ball; move to the ball; trap the ball.
Teach 10 min (50 min)	Baserunning Leaving the Batter's Box Drill Running Past First Base Drill	Teach as a group. Divide team in half for drill. Practice Leaving the Box Drill first; then run past first base.	Run slowly at first, then faster. Touch the front edge of the base. Run beyond the base. Do not leap upon the base.
Teach 10 min (60 min)	Backing-up Backing-up Drill	Teach as a group. Divide team in half for drill.	Stand about 20 ft behind the fielder. Get in the ready position. Watch the ball.
Teach 10 min (70 min)	Playing a Game Explain how a game proceeds	Explain as a group. Use the discussion in *Baseball Coaching Guide*.	Involve your players with the discussion.
Review/ Cool-down 5 min (75 min)	Easy throwing, jogging, stretching	Pair up for throwing. Jog as a group. Stretch in a group circle.	Throw easy, not fast. Jog easily; do not race. Stretch slowly; do not bounce.
Evaluation 5 min (80 min)	Review today's practice	Bring the players together.	Correct skills positively. Compliment effort and hustle. Mention time and place for next practice.

Practice Plan 3

Age: 9-12
Total time: 70 minutes

Instructional Goals
Review and practice fielding skills and backing up.
Teach bunting, rounding bases, relaying/cutting off
throws, pitching mechanics, and catching pitches.

Equipment
Balls, bats, 2 sets of bases, helmets
For the coach: Player roster, practice plans, first-aid kit

Drills
Fielding—Fielding Ground Balls Drill; Judging Fly
Balls Drill
Backing up—Short Base Drill; Backing-up Drill
Bunting—Bunt Drill
Relays/Cut-offs—Cut-off and Relay Drill
Pitching/Catching—Throwing and catching pitches
Baserunning—Rounding the Bases Drill

Component/Time	Activity/Drills	Organization	Coaching Points
Warm-up 5 min	Easy stretching, jogging, throwing	Stretch in a group circle. Jog as a group. Pair up for throws. Choose 2 players to lead warm-up.	Discuss practice and check roster during warm-up. Keep the warm-up easy.

Review/Practice
10 min (15 min)
	Fielding
	  Fielding Ground Balls Drill
	  Judging Fly Balls Drill
		Review fielding fly balls as a group. Divide team in half for drills.	Proper ready position. Watch the ball; move to the ball; trap the ball.

Teach 10 min (25 min)	Bunting Bunt Drill	Teach bunting as a group. Pair up players for drills.	Be sure to demonstrate from several angles. Square around; hold bat firm; try to catch the ball.
Teach 10 min (35 min)	Rounding the Bases Rounding the Bases Drill	Teach as a group. Divide team in half for drills.	Run only half the distance. Swing wide; turn into the base; and touch the inside corner.

Review/Practice
10 min (45 min)
	Positional Skills
	  Short Base Drill
	  Backing-up Drill
		Review coverage areas and backing-up as a group. Divide into small groups for drills.	Have players field 2 positions. Back up 10 ft behind fielder; watch the ball.

Teach 10 min (55 min)	Relays/Cut-offs Cut-off and Relay Drill	Teach as a large group. Divide into groups of 3-5 for drills.	Throw accurately, not fast. Watch the ball; trap the ball.
Teach 10 min (65 min)	Pitching/Catching Throwing and catching pitches	Teach as a group. Teach catching position first. Teach pitching mechanics second. Pair up for pitching/catching practice.	Pitching—Shift weight back, then forward; push off, throw, follow through. Slow wind-up, fast delivery. Catch—Keep back straight, feet spread apart, watch the ball.
Cool-down/ Evaluation 5 min (70 min)	Easy throwing, jogging, stretching	Choose 2 players to lead the cool-down. Pair up for throws. Jog as a group. Stretch in a group circle.	Keep the cool-down easy; review practice during cool-down. Be constructive; mention time and place for next practice.

Practice Plan 4

Age: 9-12
Total time: 70 minutes

Instructional Goals
Review and practice hitting/bunting, pitching, and catching. Teach the skip and throw, leaving and tagging up bases, making force-outs and tag-outs, and baseball playing strategy.

Equipment
Balls, bats, 2 sets of bases, helmets
For the coach: Player roster, practice plans, first-aid kit

Drills
Hitting/Bunting—Batting Practice
Pitching/Catching—Throwing and catching pitches
Skip and Throw—Step and Throw Drill
Baserunning—Leaving Bases Drill
Force-outs/Tag-outs—Force-out/Tag-out Drill
Playing Strategy—Playing Strategy Drill

Component/Time	Activity/Drills	Organization	Coaching Points
Warm-up 5 min	Easy stretching, jogging, throwing	Warm-up as a group. Choose 2 players to lead exercises.	Warm up easily.
Teach/Practice 10 min (15 min)	The Skip and Throw Step and Throw Drill	Teach in a group. Pair up players for the drill.	Use a short, low skip. Push off the back foot. Throw accurately, not fast.
Practice 10 min (25 min)	Batting Batting practice	Divide the team in half. Each half bats on separate diamonds. Players should swing and bunt.	Batting—Watch the ball; stride into the ball; swing level. Bunting—Turn square to the ball; hold the bat firmly; try to catch the ball with the bat.
Teach/Practice 10 min (35 min)	Leaving/Tagging Up Leaving Bases Drill	Teach in a group. Divide the team in half for drills.	Do not leave before the pitcher releases the ball. Push off the base.
Teach/Practice 10 min (45 min)	Force-outs/Tag-outs Force-out/Tag-out Drill	Teach in a group. Divide the team in half for drills.	Force-outs—Move to the base; touch the base; catch the ball. Tag-outs—Stand behind the base; catch the ball; place the glove in front of the runner.
Teach/Practice 10 min (55 min)	Playing Strategy Playing Strategy Drill	Teach and drill as a group. Actively include players.	Involve players in the discussion. Stress the priority of each rule.
Review/Practice 10 min (65 min)	Pitching/Catching Hit the Mitt Drill	Review pitching and catching fundamentals as a team. Pair up for the drills. While one player pitches, the other catches.	Pitching—Stride straight ahead; swing arm straight back and forward; snap the wrist and step through. Catching—Provide a target; watch the ball; trap the ball.
Cool-down/ Evaluation 5 min (70 min)	Easy throwing, jogging, stretching	Choose 2 players to lead the cool-down. Review the practice during the cool-down.	Cool down easily. Positively correct errors; compliment effort. Mention time and place for next practice.

Practice Plan 5

Age: 9-12
Total time: 70 minutes

Instructional Goals
Review and practice the skip and throw, batting, fielding, pitching, and catching. Teach the basket catch and bunt coverage. Players select 2 positions for playing games.

Equipment
Balls, bats, 2 sets of bases, 2 sets of catching equipment, helmets
For the coach: Player roster, practice plans, first-aid kit

Drills
Skip and Throw—Skip and Throw Drill; Throw and Step Back Drill
Batting/Fielding—Batting/Fielding Drill
Pitching and Catching—Hit the Mitt Drill
Basket Catch—Basket Catch Drill
Bunt Coverage—Bunt Reaction Drill

Component/Time	Activity/Drills	Organization	Coaching Points
Warm-up 5 min	Easy stretching, jogging, throwing	Choose two players to lead the warm-up. Warm up as a group.	Warm up easily. Discuss today's practice.
Practice 15 min (20 min)	Skip and Throw Drill Throw and Step Back Drill	Pair up players a moderate distance. Combine these drills. Use the skip and throw. Step back after each catch; step forward after each miss.	Throw short and easy fly balls. Progress to more difficult flies. Watch the ball; trap the ball.
Teach 15 min (35 min)	The Basket Catch Basket Catch Drill	Teach as a group. Divide team in half for drills. Each half practices on a separate field.	Positively correct skills. Encourage good positional play.
Practice 20 min (55 min)	Batting/Fielding Batting/Fielding Drill	Divide the team in half; each half practices on separate diamonds. Each player chooses 2 positions. Pitchers and catchers move to next drill.	Throw pitches the batter can hit. Stress correct batting and fielding skills.
	Pitching/Catching Hit the Mitt Drill Shift Drill	While other players field and bat, the pitchers and catchers work together. Teach catchers to shift and block low pitches.	Show catchers how to wear the equipment. Stress accuracy and catching pitches.
Teach/Practice 10 min (65 min)	Bunt Coverage Bunt Reaction Drill	Teach as a group. Divide team in half for the drills.	Charge the ball; call for the ball; back up players and bases.
Cool-down/ Evaluation 5 min (70 min)	Easy throwing, jogging, stretching	Choose 2 players to lead the cool-down as a group. Review the practice during the cool-down.	Cool down easily. Review skills that need improvement. Mention time and place for next practice.

Practice Plan 6

Instructional Goals
Practice baseball playing skills in a practice game. Review the skills of fielding, baserunning, and pitching. Teach catchers to block pitches.

Equipment
Balls, bats, 2 sets of bases, helmets, 2 sets of catching equipment
For the coach: Player roster, practice plans, first-aid kit

Drills
Fielding and Baserunning—Game Situation Drill
Pitching—Hit the Mitt Drill
Catching—Shift Drill

Component/Time	Activity/Drills	Organization	Coaching Points
Warm-up 5 min	Easy stretching, jogging, throwing	Choose 2 players to lead the warm-up. Warm up as a group.	Warm up easily. Discuss today's practice during the warm-up.
Practice 20 min (25 min)	Fielding and Baserunning Game Simulation Drill	Practice as a team, except for pitchers and catchers. Rotate players as fielders and runners.	Watch for good fielding technique. Correct poor baserunning technique.
	Pitching and Catching Hit the Mitt Drill Shift Drill	While other players field and run, pitchers and catchers practice together on another diamond.	Stress accuracy of the pitches, and catching the ball.
Practice 40 min (65 min)	Practice Game Practice Game Drill	Divide the team in half. Let each player field 2 positions. An inning ends when each player has batted.	Provide constructive advice for playing the game. Correct skills. Let them have fun.
Cool-down/ Evaluation 5 min (70 min)	Easy throwing, jogging, stretching	Choose 2 players to lead the exercises. Cool down as a group. Review the practice.	Tell them what to work on to play a game. Mention time and place of next practice.

Practice Plan 7

Instructional Goals
Practice fielding skills, batting positional skills, and team defense. Teach the skill of sliding.

Equipment
Balls, bats, 2 sets of bases, catching equipment, materials to practice sliding
For the coach: Player roster, practice plans, first-aid kit

Drills
Fielding/Batting—Batting/Fielding Drill
Team Defense/Positional Skills—Relay and Cut-Off Drill; Individual Skills Drill
Baserunning—Practice sliding

Component/Time	Activity/Drills	Organization	Coaching Points
Warm-up 5 min	Easy stretching, jogging, throwing	Choose 2 players to lead the warm-up. Warm up as a group. Discuss today's practice.	Warm up easily.
Practice 15 min (20 min)	Fielding/Batting Batting/Fielding Drill	Practice as a group. Have each player practice 2 positions. Rotate batters and fielders.	Watch for positional play, backing up, and making outs. Correct batting and fielding mechanics.
Practice 15 min (35 min)	Positional Skills Individual Position Drill	Divide the team in half. Each group practices on separate diamonds. Each player practices 2 positions.	Correct positional play from the practice game.
Practice 15 min (50 min)	Team Defense Relay and Cut-off Drill Bunt Reaction Drill	Divide the team in half. Each group practices on separate diamonds.	Use the skip and throw for relays. Charge and call for bunts.
Teach 15 min (65 min)	Sliding Practice sliding	Teach and practice as a group. Wet down grass or plastic. (This is a fun drill.)	Bend the back leg; sit down on the thigh and rear; keep the hands held up.
Cool-down/ Evaluation 5 min (70 min)	Usual cool-down if players are dry; if wet, dry off and end practice.	Cool down as a group. Review today's practice.	Mention time and place for next practice.

Practice Plan 8

Instructional Goals
Practice fielding, catching, and sliding, and prepare for a practice game by working on positional skills. Play a practice game.

Equipment
Balls, bats, 4 helmets, 2 sets of bases, 2 sets of catching equipment
For the coach: Player roster, practice plans, first-aid kit

Drills
Fielding—Outfield Ground Ball-Fly Ball Drill; Infield Teamwork Drill
Pitching/Catching—Pitching and catching practice
Baserunning—Sliding practice
Positional Skills—Individual Position Drill

Component/Time	Activity/Drills	Organization	Coaching Points
Warm-up 5 min	Easy stretching, jogging, throwing	Choose 2 players to lead the warm-up. Discuss today's practice.	Warm up easily.

Practice 10 min (15 min)	Fielding
	   Outfield Ground Ball-Fly Ball Drill
	   Infield Teamwork Drill
		Divide the infielders and outfielders. Move outfielders to the outfield; move infielders to their positions. Pitchers and catchers practice together.	Outfield—Keep the ball in front; trap the ball. Infield—Move to the ball; back up; cover positional areas.

Practice 10 min (25 min)	Baserunning Sliding practice	Divide the team in 3 groups. Rotate groups to second, third, and home. Practice sliding at each base.	Keep the hands up; bend back leg and sit down on rear.
Practice 10 min (35 min)	Positional Skills Individual Position Drill	Bring the team together. Position 2 players at each position.	Emphasize positional coverage and hustle.
Practice 30 min (65 min)	Practice Game Drill	Divide the team into 2 groups. Each inning is over when each player has batted.	Let players have fun. Provide advice for team play. Correct skill mechanics.
Cool-down/ Evaluation 5 min (70 min)	Easy throwing, jogging, stretching	Choose 2 players to lead the cool-down. Review today's practice.	Cool down easily. Mention skills to work on before the first game Mention time and place of first game.

Practice Plan 1

Age: 13 and up
Total time: 80 minutes

Instructional Goals
Teach the fundamental skills of throwing, catching, fielding, and batting. Introduce the players to playing positions and baseball rules.

Equipment
Balls, bats, 2 sets of bases, helmets
For the coach: Player roster, practice plans, first-aid kit

Drills
Throwing—Ball Grip Drill; Throwing Action Drill
Catching—Throwing and catching
Fielding—Fielding Position Drill; Fielding Ground Balls Drill
Batting—Swinging the Bat Drill
Baseball Rules—Playing Rules Drill

Component/Time	Activity/Drills	Organization	Coaching Points
Introduction 5 min	Introduce yourself and other coaches. Check the roster. Talk about how you will coach the team.	Bring the players together.	Be enthusiastic. Let them know you care about learning skills and about having fun.
Warm-up 5 min (10 min)	Easy stretching, jogging, throwing	Stretch in a group circle. Jog as a group. Pair up for throws and stand apart a moderate distance.	Lead and demonstrate from inside the circle. Stretch slowly; do not bounce. Jog easily; do not race. Do not throw fast.
Teach/Practice 10 min (20 min)	Throwing Motion Ball Grip Drill Throwing Action Drill	Teach in a group. Pair up players for drills.	Emphasize the grip, arm swing, stride, and follow-through. Throw accurately.
Teach/Practice 10 min (30 min)	Catch Throws Throw and catch	Teach in a group. Pair up for drill.	Present how to wear and use the glove. Watch the ball; trap the ball.
Teach/Practice 10 min (40 min)	Fielding Fielding Position Drill Fielding Ground Drill	Teach in a group. Practice fielding position individually. Pair up for fielding ground balls.	Emphasize proper leg and hand position. Move to the ball; watch the ball; trap the ball.
Teach/Practice 10 min (50 min)	Batting Simulating Swings Drill Hitting Off a Tee Drill	Teach in a group. Pair up for drills; players alternate swinging and watching for correct form. Spread apart and hit off a tee into fence or net.	Present proper grip, stance, stride, arm swing, and follow-through. Watch the ball.
Teach/Practice 10 min (60 min)	Positional Coverage Areas Move players through positions	Teach in a group. Rotate players through each position on the field.	Stress knowing the playing areas and the responsibilities of each position.
Teach 10 min (70 min)	Baseball Game Rules Playing Rules Drill	Conduct question-and-answer session as a group. Involve your players in the activity.	Explain the rules simply and clearly. Let your players show you their answers.
Teach/Cool-down 5 min (75 min)	Easy throwing, jogging, stretching	Pair up for throws. Jog as a group. Stretch in a group circle. Lead stretches from inside the circle.	Throw easy, not fast. Jog easily; do not race. Stretch slowly; do not bounce.
Evaluation 5 min (80 min)	Review today's practice	Bring the players together.	Correct skills positively. Mention time and place for next practice.

Practice Plan 2

Age: 13 and up
Total time: 90 minutes

Instructional Goals
Review and practice throwing, catching, and batting. Teach fielding fly balls, running to first base, rounding the bases, backing up, and how to play a game.

Equipment
Balls, bats, 2 sets of bases
For the coach: Player roster, practice plans, first-aid kit

Drills
Throwing/Catching—Throw and catch; Throw and Step Back Drill
Batting—Hit Easy Pitches Drill; Simulating Swings Drill
Fielding—Judging Fly Balls Drill
Baserunning—Leaving the Batter's Box Drill; Running Past First Base Drill
Backing Up—Backing Up Fielders Drill

Component/Time	Activity/Drills	Organization	Coaching Points
Introduction 5 min	Review the coaches' and players' names. Check the roster. Review your coaching philosophy.	Bring the players together.	Be enthusiastic. Let them know you care about learning skills and about having fun.
Review/Warm-up 5 min (10 min)	Easy stretching, jogging, throwing	Stretch in a group circle. Jog as a group. Pair up for throws and stand apart a moderate distance.	Lead and demonstrate stretches from inside the circle. Stretch slowly; do not bounce. Jog easily; do not race. Throw easy, not fast.
Review/Practice 10 min (20 min)	Throwing/Catching Throw and catch Throw and Step Back Drill	Review throwing and catching fundamentals as a group. Pair up for drills.	Throwing—Proper grip, stride, follow-through. Catching—Glove control; watch and trap the ball.
Review/Practice 10 min (30 min)	Batting Swinging the Bat Drill Hit Easy Pitches Drill	Review as a group. Pair up for drills. Spread players apart a safe distance.	Proper grip; swing level; watch the ball; stride forward and follow through.
Teach 15 min (45 min)	Fielding Fly Balls Judging Fly Balls Drill	Teach as a group. Divide team in half for drill.	Watch the ball; move to the ball; trap the ball.
Teach 10 min (55 min)	Baserunning Leaving the Batter's Box Drill Running Past First Base Drill	Teach as a group. Divide team in half for drill. Practice the Leaving the Box Drill first; then run past first base.	Run slowly at first, then faster. Touch the front edge of the base; run beyond the base. Do not leap upon the base.
Teach 10 min (65 min)	Backing Up Backing Up Drill	Teach as a group. Divide team in half for drill.	Stand about 20 ft behind the fielder. Get in the ready position. Watch the ball.
Teach 15 min (80 min)	Playing a Game Explain how a game proceeds	Explain as a group. Use the discussion in the *Baseball Coaching Guide.*	Involve your players in the discussion.
Review/ Cool-down 5 min (85 min)	Easy throwing, jogging, stretching	Pair up for throwing. Jog as a group. Stretch in a group.	Throw easy, not fast. Jog easily; do not race. Stretch slowly; do not bounce.
Evaluation 5 min (90 min)	Review today's practice	Bring the players together.	Be positive; compliment effort and hustle. Provide constructive feedback.

Practice Plan 3

Age: 13 and up
Total time: 95 minutes

Instructional Goals
Review and practice backing up players. Teach the skip and throw, the basket catch, bunting, relays and cut-offs, and pitching mechanics.

Equipment
Balls, bats, helmets
For the coach: Player roster, practice plans, first-aid kit

Drills
Throwing—Step and Throw Drill
Fielding—Basket Catch Drill
Batting—Bunt Drill
Relays/Cut-offs—Cut-off and Relay Drill
Backing Up—Backing-Up Drill
Pitching and Catching—Throwing and catching pitches

Component/Time	Activity/Drills	Organization	Coaching Points
Warm-up 5 min	Easy stretching, jogging, throwing	Stretch in a group. Jog as a group. Pair up for throws. Choose 2 players to lead warm-up.	Discuss practice and check the roster. Keep the warm-up easy.
Teach 10 min (15 min)	The Skip and Throw Step and Throw Drill	Teach as a group. Pair up for drills. Position players apart a moderate distance.	Hop low and short; push off the back foot; throw accurately.
Teach 15 min (30 min)	The Basket Catch Basket Catch Drill	Teach as a group. Divide the team in half for drill.	Watch the ball; move to the ball; trap the ball.
Teach 15 min (45 min)	Bunting Bunt Drill	Teach as a group. Pair up players for drill.	Watch the ball; square to the ball. Hold the bat firm; try to catch the ball.
Review/Practice 10 min (55 min)	Backing Up Backing-up Drill	Review as a group. Divide the team in half for the drill. Each half practices on separate diamonds.	Hustle! Back up 20 ft behind the fielder; watch the ball.
Teach 20 min (75 min)	Relays/Cut-offs Cut-off and Relay Drill	Teach as a group. Divide the team into groups of 3-5 for the drill.	Throw using the skip and throw. Throw accurately, not fast.
Teach 15 min (90 min)	Pitching/Catching Throwing and catching pitches	Teach pitching mechanics as a group. Pair up for practice.	Pitching—Shift weight back, then forward; push off, throw, follow through. Slow wind-up, fast delivery. Catching—Watch the ball; trap the ball.
Cool-down/ Evaluation 5 min (95 min)	Easy throwing, jogging, stretching	Choose 2 players to lead the cool-down. Pair up for throws; jog as a group; stretch in a group circle.	Review the practice; be positive and constructive. They learned much today. Mention time and place for next practice.

Practice Plan 4

Age: 13 and up
Total time: 90 minutes

Instructional Goals
Practice throwing, catching, and pitching. Teach leaving and tagging up a base, force-outs and tag-outs, bunt coverage, and playing strategy.

Equipment
Balls, bats, 2 sets of bases
For the coach: Player roster, practice plans, first-aid kit

Drills
Throwing/Catching—Step and Throw Drill; Throw and Step Back Drill
Pitching/Catching—Throwing and catching pitches
Leaving and Tagging Up—Leaving Bases Drill
Force-outs/Tag-outs—Force-out, Tag-out Drill
Bunt Coverage—Bunt Reaction Drill
Playing Strategy—Playing Strategy Drill

Component/Time	Activity/Drills	Organization	Coaching Points
Warm-up 5 min	Easy stretching, jogging, throwing	Choose 2 players to lead the warm-up. Warm up as a group.	Keep the warm-up easy. Discuss today's practice.
Practice 10 min (15 min)	Throwing/Catching Step and Throw Drill Throw and Step Back Drill	Pair up for drills.	Throw accurately; push off the back leg; follow through.
Teach 15 min (30 min)	Leaving/Tagging Up Leaving the Bases Drill	Teach as a group. Divide the team in half for drills. Each half practices on a separate diamond.	Leaving—Watch the ball; push off the back foot; listen to the base coach. Tagging up—Watch the ball; leave and return; listen to the base coach.
Teach 15 min (45 min)	Force-outs/Tag-outs Force-out, Tag-out Drill	Teach as a group. Divide the team in half for drill. Each half practices on separate diamonds.	Force-outs—Move to the base; touch the base; catch the ball. Tag-outs—Stand behind the base; catch the ball; place the glove in front of the runner.
Teach 10 min (55 min)	Bunt Coverage Bunt Reaction Drill	Teach as a group. Divide the team in half for the drills.	Charge the ball; call for the ball; back up players and move to the bases.
Teach 15 min (70 min)	Playing Strategy Playing Strategy Drill	Teach as a group. Use the discussion in *Baseball Coaches Guide.*	Involve players in the discussion. Stress the priority of the rules.
Practice 15 min (85 min)	Pitching/Catching Throwing and catching pitches	Pair up for the drills. Pitch from regulation distance.	Pitching—Pitch accurately; stride toward the target; follow through. Catching—Watch the ball; trap the ball.
Cool-down/ Evaluation 5 min (90 min)	Easy throwing, jogging, stretching	Choose 2 players to lead the cool-down. Cool down as a group.	Review the practice. Mention time and place for next practice. Wear proper clothing for sliding practice.

Practice Plan 5

Age: 13 and up
Total time: 90 minutes

Instructional Goals
Practice fielding skills, positional skills, pitching and catching. Teach how to place hits, slide, and make double plays.

Equipment
Balls, bats, helmets, 2 sets of catching equipment, 2 sets of bases, sliding equipment
For the coach: Player roster, practice plans, first-aid kit

Drills
Fielding—Outfield Ground Ball-Fly Ball Drill; Infield-Outfield Drill
Positional Skills—Individual Position Drill; Infield and Outfield Drill
Pitching/Catching—Hit the Mitt Drill
Batting—Batting/Fielding Drill
Baserunning—Sliding practice
Team Defense—Receiving Tosses Drill; Double Play Practice Drill

Component/Time	Activity/Drills	Organization	Coaching Points
Warm-up 5 min	Easy stretching, jogging, throwing	Choose 2 players to lead the warm-up.	Discuss today's practice.

Practice
15 min (20 min)
	Fielding
	  Outfield Ground Ball-Fly Ball Drill
	  Infield and Outfield Drill
	    (infield only)
		Divide the infielders, outfielders, pitchers, and catchers. Fielders practice fielding; pitchers and catchers practice pitching.	Outfield—Move to the ball; watch the ball, and keep the ball in front. Infield—Move to the ball; trap the ball; throw accurately.

	Pitching/Catching Hit the Mitt Drill	Separate the pitchers/catchers from the team. Practice on a separate field while the fielders practice together.	Pitching—Proper arm swing, stride, wrist snap, and follow-through. Catching—Present a good target; watch and trap the ball.
Teach 15 min (35 min)	Batting-Placing Hits Batting/Fielding Drill	Teach as a group. Divide team in half for drill. Each half practices on a separate field.	Use the contact angle to direct hits. Time the pitch; step open or closed.

Teach
20 min (55 min)
	Double Plays
	  Receiving Tosses Drill
	  Double Play Practice Drill
		Teach as a group. Divide team in half for practice. Have both infielders and outfielders practice double plays.	Toss the ball easily. Touch and step away from the base. Throw accurately to first base.

Practice
15 min (70 min)
	Positional Play
	  Individual Position Drill
	  Infield and Outfield Drill
		Divide team in half. Each coach conducts one drill on separate fields. Rotate players after 7 min.	Be aware of the coverage areas and responsibilities. Encourage hustle and communication.

Teach 15 min (85 min)	Sliding Sliding practice	Set up the field for sliding (wet plastic, grass, or loose dirt). Demonstrate and teach as a group.	Bend the back leg; sit down on the thigh and hip; hold the hands up.
Cool-down/ Evaluation 5 min (90 min)	Easy throwing, jogging, stretching	Cool down if the players are not wet. If they are wet, review the practice and dismiss.	Review the practice. Point out good skills and those which need work. Practice game for next session.

Practice Plan 6

Instructional Goals
Practice the fundamental skills in a practice game. Review and practice fielding, batting, baserunning, pitching, and catching to prepare for the game. Teach catchers how to shift and block pitches.

Equipment
Balls, bats, 2 sets of catching equipment, 2 sets of bases, helmets
For the coach: Player roster, practice plans, first-aid kit

Drills
Fielding—Infield and Outfield Drill
Batting—Bunt Drill; Batting practice
Baserunning—Running the Bases Drill
Pitching/Catching—Shift Drill; Hit the Mitt Drill
Practice Game—Practice Game Drill

Component/Time	Activity/Drills	Organization	Coaching Points
Warm-up 5 min	Easy throwing, jogging, stretching	Choose 2 players to lead the warm-up.	Warm up easily. Discuss today's practice.
Practice 15 min (20 min)	Fielding Infield and Outfield Drill	Divide the team in half. Separate the pitchers and catchers. Pitchers and catchers practice together.	Move to the ball; watch the ball. Communicate with other fielders. Throw accurately.
Teach/Practice 15 min (35 min)	Pitching/Catching Shift Drill Hit the Mitt Drill	Separate the pitchers and catchers. Teach catchers to shift and block pitches. Practice pitching and catching.	Pitching—Stress accuracy. Catching—Shift with the hips; block pitches with the mitt.
	Batting Bunt Drill Batting practice	Divide the team in half. Practice on separate diamonds.	Bunt—Square to the ball; try to catch the ball; place the bunt. Hitting—Swing level; step into the pitch; watch the ball.
Practice 10 min (45 min)	Baserunning Running the Bases Drill	Divide the team in half. Practice on separate diamonds.	Step toward first base. Do not leap upon the bases. Swing wide, turn in, and touch the corner.
Practice 40 min (85 min)	Practice Practice Game Drill	Divide the team in half.	Stress proper mechanics, team communication, and backing up. Let them have fun.
Cool-down/ Evaluation 5 min (90 min)	Easy throwing, jogging, stretching	Choose 2 players to lead the cool-down.	Review the practice. Mention time and place of next practice.

Practice Plan 7

Age: 13 and up
Total time: 75 minutes

Instructional Goals
Practice fielding, batting, team defense, pitching, and catching.

Equipment
Balls, bats, helmets, 2 sets of catching equipment, 2 sets of bases
For the coach: Player roster, practice plans, first-aid kit

Drills
Fielding—Infield and Outfield Drill; Outfield Ground Ball-Fly Ball Drill
Batting—Batting practice
Team Defense—Game Situation Drill; Backing-up Drill
Pitching/Catching—Shift Drill; Throwing and catching pitches

Component/Time	Activity/Drills	Organization	Coaching Points
Warm-up 5 min	Easy stretching, jogging, throwing	Choose 2 players to lead the warm-up.	Discuss today's practice. Keep the warm-up easy.

Practice 15 min (20 min)	Fielding
	  Infield and Outfield Drill (infielders)
	  Outfield Ground Ball-Fly Ball Drill
		Divide the infielders, outfielders, pitchers, and catchers. Infielders practice together. Outfielders practice together. Pitchers and catchers practice pitching.	Use the glove correctly. Trap the ball; keep the ball in front.

	Pitching/Catching
	  Shift Drill
	  Hit the Mitt Drill
		Catchers practice shifting. Pitchers practice pitching and catching.	Catching—Provide a target. Move quickly to block pitches. Pitching—Stress control; watch the stride and release; step toward the target; follow through.

Practice 30 min (50 min)	Batting
	  Bunt Drill
	  Batting practice
		Divide the team in half. Practice drills separately, and switch players after 15 min.	Square to bunt and place the ball. Swing level and watch the ball.

Practice 20 min (70 min)	Team Defense
	  Game Situation Drill
	  Backing-up Drill
		Divide the team in half. Practice each drill on a separate diamond. Switch after 10 min.	Stress communication, hustle, and knowing where to throw. Back up about 10 ft behind the fielder.

Cool-down/ Evaluation 5 min (75 min)	Easy throwing, jogging, stretching	Choose two players to lead the cool-down.	Review the practice; compliment their effort and skills. Next session is a practice game.

Practice Plan 8

Age: 13 and up
Total time: 90 minutes

Instructional Goals
Practice fielding, baserunning, team defense, pitching and catching in preparation for a practice game.

Equipment
Balls, bats, helmets, 2 sets of bases, 2 sets of catching equipment
For the coach: Player roster, practice plans, first-aid kit

Drills
Fielding—Fielding Ground Balls Drill; Judging Fly Balls Drill
Baserunning—Running the Bases Drill
Team Defense—Cut-off and Relay Drill; Backing-up Drill
Pitching/Catching—Hit the Mitt Drill
Practice Game—Practice Game Drill

Component/Time	Activity/Drills	Organization	Coaching Points
Warm-up 5 min	Easy stretching, jogging, throwing	Choose 2 players to lead the warm-up.	Discuss today's practice.
Practice 20 min (25 min)	Fielding Fielding Ground Balls Drill Judging Fly Balls Drill	Divide the team in half. Each half practices on a separate field. Switch players after 10 min. Separate pitchers and catchers.	Watch the ball and move to the ball; keep the ball in front; trap the ball.
	Pitching/Catching	Separate pitchers and catchers from other fielders. Pitch and catch in a separate area.	Pitching—Pitch accurately. Catching—Keep the ball in front; block poor pitches.
Practice 10 min (35 min)	Baserunning Running the Bases Drill	Divide the team in half and practice on separate diamonds.	Run fast, but under control. Do not leave the base early.
Practice 10 min (45 min)	Team Defense Cut-off and Relay Drill Backing-up Drill	Divide the team into groups of 3 to 5 players. Switch drills after 5 min.	Throw accurately; use the skip and throw. Back up 10 ft behind the fielder. Watch the ball.
Practice 40 min (85 min)	Practice Game Practice Game Drill	Divide the team in half.	Encourage and compliment hustle and effort. Let them have fun. Correct skills constructively.
Cool-down/ Evaluation 5 min (90 min)	Easy throwing, jogging, stretching	Choose 2 players to lead the cool-down.	Review the practice. Mention time and place of first game.

Chapter 13:
Playing Games and Evaluating Performances

Game time should be the most enjoyable and fun part of the season—for coaches and players. If you and your players have worked hard during practices, you will be ready to have fun playing well and competing with another team. Winning is important, but one team will win and one team must lose. We urge you to keep winning in perspective by stressing the fun of playing well and competing rather than the outcome of the game.

Getting ready for each game does require a little extra work by the coach. This chapter covers (a) warming up for games, (b) keeping game score, (c) establishing a batting order, and (d) what to do after each game.

Warming Up for Games

A proper warm-up is just as important when preparing to play a game as it is when preparing to practice. In fact, the pregame warm-up should be similar to the warm-up during practices. Be sure your players exercise the arms, legs, stomach, and back. Begin with easy exercises and progress to more strenuous exercises.

The pregame warm-up should include practicing skills specific to the position your players are assigned. Tell your players which positions they will play at the practice before each game or well in advance of the game. Also, allow enough time for players who do not start the game to warm up prior to entering the game. Traditionally, pitchers are the only players who warm up after the game begins. However, in order to play well and prevent injuries, every player should warm up properly before entering the game.

How can you make sure your players are warmed up and ready to play when you need them? A good method is to determine which positions each will play, how many innings he or she will play that position, when substitutes will enter the game, and which positions the substitutes will play. By planning your game strategy well ahead of time, each player will be able to play several innings, know when he or she will enter the game, and be motivated to warm up properly.

The Batting Order

In addition to planning which position each player will be assigned, it is a good idea to plan the batting order. If you are not familiar with how to determine the batting order, some guidelines are listed below. These guidelines consider the abilities of each batter and how these abilities influence game-playing strategy.

- Assign the *leadoff* batting position to a player who has a good eye for the strike zone and is not afraid to swing, but who is also willing to wait for a walk.
- The *second* batter should be a good bunter or be able to contact the ball well and be a good base runner.
- The *third* batter will often be in position to move other players around the bases or will need to get on with 2 outs. This means the third batter should be able to place the ball and run the bases well.
- The *fourth* batter is often called the *clean-up* batter because two or three runners may be on base, and the bases will need to be cleared or cleaned up. Consequently, the fourth batter should be able to hit the ball hard.
- The *fifth* batter can come to bat with 1 or 2 outs and two or more runners on base; he or she should also be a hard hitter.
- The *sixth* batter can be considered a second leadoff batter and may often be the first batter in a new inning.
- Because the *seventh* batter follows the second leadoff batter, he or she should have abilities similar to the second batter.
- The *eighth* batter should have abilities similar to the third batter.
- The *ninth* batter is traditionally the poorest batter. Because many older players specialize in their positions, pitchers tend to be poor hitters and are often scheduled as the last batter. However, in youth baseball, the pitcher is usually a good athlete who can hit well and should be placed wherever he or she will most benefit the team.

Keeping Score

Keeping score will be relatively easy if you become familiar with a few abbreviations. Many scorebooks and rulebooks will help you by providing examples of how to score a game. The following abbreviations are commonly used to designate player positions, walks, outs, baserunning, and scoring.

Numbers Designating Defensive Positions

1—Pitcher	6—Shortstop
2—Catcher	7—Left Fielder
3—1st Baseman	8—Center Fielder
4—2nd Baseman	9—Right Fielder
5—3rd Baseman	

Abbreviations Indicating Actions

W—Walk (BB—Base on balls)	TP—Triple Play
	S—Stolen Base
K—Strike Out	OS—Out Stealing
Kc—Called Third Strike	FC—Fielder's Choice
E—Error	SF—Sacrifice Fly
B—Balk	AB—Times at Bat
O—Out	R—Runs
FL—Foul Out	H—Hits
FO—Force-Out	RBI—Runs Batted In
H—Sacrifice	G—Ground Ball (for unassisted infield outs)
PB—Passed Ball	
WP—Wild Pitch	
HP—Hit by Pitch	F—Fly Ball
DP—Double Play	

What to Do After Each Game

As the season progresses, you will become more familiar with the abilities of your players and with your abilities as a coach. Each game is a sort of measuring stick indicating the abilities of your players and of your coaching ability and will give you some direction for planning future practices. As a coach you have three specific tasks after each game: (a) to evaluate playing ability, (b) to refine skills, and (c) to introduce new skills.

Evaluate Playing Ability

Take some time after each game to evaluate the playing ability of your athletes and to determine on which skills to work. Decide if overall team play was above, below, or equal to the team's ability for this stage of the season. Determining what your players need to work on may or may not be obvious. Some errors are easily detectable while others are not.

Coaching Aids

Two coaching aids have been developed to help you evaluate playing ability and to monitor the progress of your team. These are the Individual Skills Checklist and the Team Performance Checklist. The Individual Skills Checklist will help you monitor the skill development of each player, practice by practice, throughout the season and during games. The Team Performance Checklist will help you and your assistants evaluate the quality of team performance during games by identifying errors and evaluating possible causes for the errors. Outlines of these coaching aids can be found in Appendix C. Make copies of these checklists and use them during practices and games to chart the progress of your team.

Refine Skills

Refining skills can be a difficult and time-consuming process. Most often errors are not caused by complex, technical movement problems, but by simple, basic mistakes. Refer to the Baseball Coaching Guide for an analysis of skill techniques and take steps to correct the skills as soon as possible. Improvements often come slowly, but as the pieces are put together, both you and your players will receive a great deal of personal satisfaction.

Introduce New Skills

As the season progresses and your players become more skilled and experienced, you may want to teach more advanced skills. For example, you can add bunting to the offense, double-play coverage and bunt coverage to the defense, or add other skills not covered in *Coaching Baseball Effectively*. When you do teach more advanced skills, be sure not to go too far beyond the ability of your players. Remember to challenge them to perform those new skills that they are physically and mentally capable of mastering.

Appendices

Appendix A: Baseball Rules

These condensed rules are intended to provide you with the basic baseball rules in a simplified format. They are not intended to replace any official rulebook adopted by any national or local organization. Where discrepancies exist, you should refer to the official rule book of your league or national organization, and consider it authoritative.

Game Preliminaries

1. Before the game begins the umpire should be sure that all playing lines are marked with noncaustic lime, chalk, or other white material easily distinguishable from the ground or grass.
2. Receive a supply of baseballs that meets league specifications and standards. The umpire shall be the sole judge of fitness of the balls to be used in the game.
3. Players should not intentionally discolor or damage the ball.
4. A player in the starting line-up who has been removed for a substitute may reenter the game once in any position in the batting order.
5. The pitcher must pitch to the first batter or any substitute batter until the batter is put out or reaches first base unless the pitcher becomes injured and is removed from the game.
6. The manager must immediately notify the umpire-in-chief of any substitution and state the substitute's place in the batting order.

7. The umpire-in-chief, after having been notified, should immediately announce each substitution.
8. Players, managers, and coaches should not address, or mingle with spectators, nor sit in the stands during a game.
9. The managers of both teams should agree on the fitness of the playing field before the game starts.
10. The umpire-in-chief is the sole judge as to whether and when play shall be suspended during a game because of weather conditions or of the unfit condition of the playing field.
11. Play is suspended when the umpire calls "Time." Play resumes when the umpire calls "Play."

Starting and Ending the Game

1. The home team manager and the visiting manager give the batting order to the umpire-in-chief.
2. Players of the home team take the defensive positions, the first batter of the visiting team takes position in the batter box, the umpire calls "Play," and the game begins.
3. When the ball is put in play at the start of or during a game, all fielders other than the catcher must be on fair territory; the catcher must be in the catcher's box.
4. The batting order must be followed throughout the game unless a player is substituted for another. Substitutes must take the place

of the replaced player's position in the batting order.

5. Two coaches may be positioned by the offensive team during its time at bat, one near first base and one near third base.

6. A manager, coach, or player ejected from a game must leave the field immediately and take no further part in that game.

7. One run is scored each time a runner legally advances to and touches first, second, third, and home base before three players are put out to end the inning.

8. Tie games halted due to weather, curfew, or light failure are resumed from the exact point at which they were halted in the original game.

9. Protest shall be considered only when based on the violation or interpretation of a playing rule or the use of ineligible player. No protest shall be considered on a decision involving an umpire's judgment.

Putting the Ball in Play

1. After the umpire calls "Play," the ball is alive and in play and remains alive and in play until the umpire calls "Time." While the ball is dead, no player may be put out, no bases may be run, and no runs may be scored.

2. The pitcher pitches to the batter who chooses to strike or not to strike at the ball.

3. One run is scored for the runner's team when a batter becomes a runner and touches all bases legally.

4. After three offensive players are legally put out, that team takes the field, and the opposing team becomes the offensive team.

5. The ball becomes dead and runners advance one base, or return to the bases, without liability to be put out when
   - a pitched ball touches the batter or the batter's clothing while in a legal batting position;
   - the plate umpire interferes with the catcher's throw (if the catcher's throw gets

the runner out, the out stands, no umpire interference);
   - a balk is committed;
   - a ball is illegally batted either fair or foul;
   - a foul ball is not caught (umpires shall not put the ball in play until all runners have retouched their bases); and
   - a fair ball touches a runner or an umpire on fair territory before it touches an infielder, including the pitcher, or touches an umpire before it has passed an infielder other than the pitcher. A runner hit by a fair batted ball is out.

The Batter

1. Each player of the offensive team must bat in the order that his or her name appears in the team's batting order. The first batter in each inning, after the first inning, is the player whose name follows that of the last player who legally completed a time at bat in the preceding inning.

2. The batter takes position with both feet in the batter's box and must not leave that position after the pitcher comes to set position, or starts a windup.

3. A batter is out when
   - a fair or foul fly ball is legally caught by a fielder;
   - a third strike is legally caught by the catcher;
   - a bunting foul is made on a third strike;
   - an infield fly is called;
   - the batter attempts to hit a third strike and is touched by the ball;
   - a fair ball touches the batter before touching a fielder;
   - the bat hits the ball a second time in fair territory;
   - the batter-runner or first base is tagged before the batter-runner touches first base; and
   - a runner intentionally interferes with a fielder who is attempting to complete any play.

4. Batting out of turn:
   - A batter is called out, on appeal, when failing to bat in proper order, and another batter completes a time at bat in place of the proper batter.
   - When an improper batter becomes a runner or is put out, and the defensive team appeals to the umpire before the first pitch to the next batter of either team or before any play or attempted play, the umpire declares the proper batter out and nullifies offensive play.
   - When an improper batter becomes a runner or is put out, and a pitch is made to the next batter of either team before an appeal is made, the improper batter becomes the proper batter, and the results of his or her time at bat are legal.
   - When the proper batter is called out for failing to bat in turn, the next batter is the batter following the proper batter who was called out; an improper batter becomes a proper batter when no appeal is made before the next pitch, and the next batter is then the batter following the improper batter.

The Runner

1. A runner acquires the right to an unoccupied base when that runner touches it before being put out. The runner is then entitled to it until put out or forced to vacate it for another runner legally entitled to that base.
2. In advancing, a runner must touch first, second, third, and home base in order. If forced to return, the runner must retouch all bases in reverse order.
3. Two runners may not occupy a base, but if two runners are touching the same base, the following runner is out when tagged because the preceding runner is entitled to the base.
4. Each runner may advance one base when (a) there is a balk and (b) the batter is walked, forcing the runner to vacate the base.

5. Each runner including the batter-runner may advance
   - to home base if a fair ball goes out of the playing field in flight, and the runner touches all bases legally;
   - two bases, if a fielder deliberately touches a thrown ball with a cap, mask or any part of the uniform removed from the body;
   - two bases, if a fielder deliberately throws a glove at and touches a thrown ball;
   - two bases, if a fair ball bounces or is deflected into the stands outside the first or third base foul lines, or if it goes through or is trapped in a fence, scoreboard, or bushes;
   - two bases when a thrown ball goes out of play; and
   - one base, if a ball, pitched to the batter or thrown by the pitcher on the pitcher's plate, goes out of the playing field.
6. A runner is out when
   - running more than 3 ft away from a direct line between bases to avoid being tagged;
   - intentionally interfering with a thrown ball, or hindering a fielder attempting to make a play;
   - off a base and tagged with the ball;
   - tagged with the ball, or the base is touched with the ball before the runner tags up on a fly ball; and
   - touched by a fair ball in fair territory before the ball has touched or passed an infielder.
7. Unless there are 2 outs, a following runner is not affected by a preceding runner's failure to touch or retouch a base. If the preceding runner is the third out, no runners following the preceding runner score, and if the third out is the result of a force play, neither the preceding nor the following runners score.

The Pitcher

1. Pitchers must take signs from the catcher while standing with at least one foot on the rubber.

2. At any time during the pitcher's preliminary movements and until the natural pitching motion commits the pitcher to pitch, he or she may throw to any base provided he or she steps directly toward the base.

3. If the pitcher removes the pivot foot from contact with the pitcher's plate by stepping backward with that foot, the pitcher becomes an infielder.

4. The pitcher must *not*
   • touch the mouth or lips with the pitching hand within the 10 ft pitching circle;
   • intentionally delay the game by throwing the ball to players other than the catcher when the batter is in position, except in an attempt to throw out a runner; or
   • intentionally throw to hit the batter.

5. It is a balk when
   • the pitcher is on the pitching rubber and begins but does not complete the pitch;
   • the pitcher, while touching the plate, fakes a throw to first base and does not complete the throw;
   • the pitcher is on the pitching rubber and does not step directly toward a base before throwing to that base;
   • the pitcher, while touching the pitching rubber, throws or fakes a throw to an unoccupied base, except to make a play;
   • the pitcher makes an illegal pitch;
   • the pitcher pitches the ball without facing the batter;
   • the pitcher makes a pitching motion without touching the pitching rubber;
   • the pitcher unnecessarily delays the game;
   • the pitcher fakes a pitch;
   • the pitcher, while touching the pitching rubber, drops the ball; or
   • the pitcher, while giving an intentional base on balls, pitches when the catcher is not in the catcher's box.

Appendix B: Instructional Schedule and Practice Plan Outlines

4-Week Instructional Schedule for Youth Baseball

Goal: To help players learn and practice the individual and team skills needed to play a regulation game after 4 weeks.

T(10): Teach skill for first time in 10 min.
P(10): Practice or drill the skill for 10 min.

*: These skill components are practiced during the drills for this playing category.

Skills	Week 1 Day 1	Day 2	Week 2 Day 3	Day 4	Week 3 Day 5	Day 6	Week 4 Day 7	Day 8	Time in Minutes
Throwing/Catching									
Fielding									
Batting									
Baserunning									
Positional Skills									
Team Defense									
Game Play									
Pitching									
Catching									

Practice Plan #____

Total time: _____ minutes

Instructional Goals   *Drills*

Equipment

Component/Time	Activity/Drills	Organization	Coaching Points

Appendix C: Individual Skills Checklist and Team Performance Checklist Outlines

Individual Skills Checklist

Practice (game) _____

Evaluate skills as: Good, O.K., Needs work

Name	Hitting/ Bunting	Running Bases	Throwing/ Catching	Position/ Fielding	Team-Play	Comments/ Suggestions

Team Performance Checklist

Game _____
Evaluate skills as: Good, O.K., Needs work

Team Play	Good	O.K.	Needs Work	Additional Comments
Hustle				
Back-up play				
Relay and cut-off				
Baserunning				
Communication				
Following instructions				
Pitching				
Batting				
Coaching Performance				
Base coaching				
Attitude				
Instructions and comments				

Appendix D:
Coaching Baseball
Effectively
Evaluation

Tell Us What You Think

It is our commitment at ACEP to provide coaches with the most complete, accurate, and useful information available. Our authors, consultants, and editors are continuously searching for new ideas and are constantly seeking to improve our materials. Now that you have read and studied this book, it is your turn to tell us what you liked and did not like about it. Please take a few minutes to complete the following survey and send it to: ACEP, Box 5076, Champaign, IL 61820.

Book Evaluation for
Coaching Baseball Effectively

Instructions: For each statement mark the spaces in the left-hand column which correspond to what you think of this book. We are interested in your opinions so feel free to mark more than one response to each statement.

1. The organization of this book
___ (a) presents material in an easy-to-understand progression
___ (b) is helpful
___ (c) is confusing

2. The material presented in this book is
___ (a) easy to read and understand
___ (b) difficult to read and understand
___ (c) too simple
___ (d) too complex

3. Figures and illustrations are
___ (a) helpful
___ (b) distracting
___ (c) technically correct
___ (d) technically incorrect
___ (e) confusing

4. Coaching points and teaching progressions
___ (a) highlight material in the book well
___ (b) progress from basic to advanced concepts
___ (c) are helpful
___ (d) are distracting
___ (e) are too repetitive

5. Drills
___ (a) need illustrations
___ (b) are helpful
___ (c) are confusing
___ (d) are too advanced for beginning players
___ (e) are too simple for beginning players
___ (f) are easy to use
___ (g) are difficult to use

6. Instructional schedules are
___ (a) helpful
___ (b) easy to understand
___ (c) difficult to understand

7. Practice plans are
___ (a) helpful
___ (b) confusing
___ (c) too basic
___ (d) too advanced
___ (e) easy to use
___ (f) difficult to use

8. Coaching aids are
___ (a) helpful
___ (b) not helpful
___ (c) easy to use
___ (d) difficult to use

Yes No
___ 9. **I feel more knowledgeable about coaching baseball to beginning athletes than I did before reading this book.**

___ 10. **I would like to attend a workshop or clinic covering the material presented in this book.**

Glossary

Backing up—Moving behind a base or player to field balls that get by the player.

Balk—An illegal pitching motion by the pitcher. A ball is credited to the batter and runners are allowed to advance one base.

Barrel—This is the fat section of the bat and is used to hit a pitched ball.

Basket catch—Catching with the glove pocket facing upward and held at or below the waist.

Battery—The duo of the pitcher and catcher.

Blocking position—The ground ball fielding position of an outfielder where the player kneels on the glove-side knee and places the mitt between the legs.

Breaking in—Conditioning a new glove by forming its shape and softening the leather.

Bunt—A method of hitting the ball by squaring with the pitcher and holding the bat so the ball is hit softly.

Checkpoint—Positions used to evaluate components or phases of a skill. The point of release is a checkpoint of the pitching motion.

Closed stance—The batting position in which the front foot is close to the inside of the batter's box and the back foot is toward the outside of the batter's box.

Cut off—To catch a ball before it reaches a particular base. The shortstop may cut off a throw to third base.

Deep—To play the back part of the infield (for infielders) or the back part of the outfield (for outfielders).

Follow-through—The movement of the body resulting from a well performed skill such as throwing, swinging, and batting.

Force-out—An out that occurs when a ball reaches a base before the runner does. A force-out is in effect when a runner *must* advance to a base.

Grip—The way a ball, bat, or other implement is held.

Guard the line—Playing close to the first or third baseline to prevent a ball from being hit directly down the line.

Handle—This is the part of the bat gripped by the batter.

Holding on—Keeping a runner on or close to a base; preventing a runner from leading off or advancing to another base.

Hop-step—Throwing the ball by taking a short skip on the back foot. This is also the skip and throw.

Infield fly rule—This rule is in effect when runners are on first and second or the bases are loaded, with less than 2 outs. Under these conditions, if a pop-up is hit to the infield or shallow outfield, the batter is automatically *out*, and the runners are not forced to advance.

Knob—This is the rounded part of the bat at the end of the handle that prevents the hand from slipping off.

Leading off—When a batter leaves a base in anticipation of running to the next base.

Open stance—The batting position in which the front foot is positioned toward the outside of the batters's box, and the back foot is positioned toward the inside of the batter's box.

Overhand throw—Throwing the ball with the arm swinging over the top of the body, as opposed to the sidearm throw. The overhand throw is more accurate than the sidearm throw.

Pull—Hitting to the opposite part of the field. A right-handed batter pulls a ball to right field. A left-handed batter pulls a ball to left field.

Ready position—The position of a player preparing to play a ball.

Relay—Using several players to throw the ball over a long distance.

Rounding—Running around a base rather than stopping at a base.

Sidearm throw—Throwing the ball with the arm swinging around the side of the body, as opposed to the overhand throw. The sidearm throw is less accurate and should be taught only after players can throw overhand well.

Shallow—Playing the front part of the infield (for infielders), or the front part of the outfield (for outfielders).

Shift—Moving the body weight. The body weight is shifted when throwing, catching, and batting. Also, catchers shift to block wild throws.

Short hop—A thrown or hit ball that lands close to a fielder and hops or bounces up quickly.

Slide—A controlled fall enabling runners to move into a base without standing up. Sliding is a good way to reach a base while avoiding a tag.

Square—To be in line and evenly facing a position, object, or person. To perform a bunt, the batter turns square to the pitcher.

Stance—The upright, standing position of a fielder or batter. The stance should provide a solid base of support.

Steal—Advancing to another base without the ball being hit or a batter being walked. A runner steals second base.

Strategy—Plans and reasons for making plays. The defense uses certain playing strategies to control the offense.

Stretch position—Pitching position where the push-off foot is in front of the pitching rubber and the lead foot is stretched out or ready to pitch. Use the stretch position when runners need to be held close to a base.

Stride—Stepping into a throw or swing. The stride should be short and controlled.

Swing—Moving the arms around the body to throw a ball or swing a bat. The batting swing moves the bat around the body.

Tag up—Touching a base after a fly ball has been caught. Base runners must tag up on caught fly balls before running to the next base.

Take in—Catching a ball while fielding ground balls or fly balls. This differs from a regular catch in that a take-in is specifically for catching a hit or rolling ball, not a thrown ball. The third baseman takes in a short hop.